Wuthering Heights

Open Guides to Literature

Series Editor: Graham Martin (Professor of Literature, The Open University)

Current titles

Graham Holderness: *Wuthering Heights*
P.N. Furbank: Pound
Graham Martin: *Great Expectations*
Roderick Watson: MacDiarmid

Titles in preparation

Angus Calder: Byron
David Pirie: Shelley
Walford Davies: Dylan Thomas
Roger Day: Larkin
Jeanette King: *Jane Eyre*
Dennis Walder: Hughes
Graham Holderness: *Women in Love*

GRAHAM HOLDERNESS

Wuthering Heights

Open University Press

Milton Keynes · *Philadelphia*

Open University Press
Open University Educational Enterprises Limited
12 Cofferidge Close
Stony Stratford
Milton Keynes MK11 1BY, England
and
242 Cherry Street
Philadelphia, PA 19106, USA

First Published 1985

British Library Cataloguing in Publication Data
Holderness, Graham
    Wuthering Heights. — (Open guides to literature)
    1. Brontë, Emily. Wuthering Heights
    I. Title   II. Series
    823'.8   PR4172.W73

ISBN 0–335–15087–X
ISBN 0–335–15073–X Pbk

Library of Congress Cataloging in Publication Data
Main entry under title:
Holderness, Graham.
    Wuthering Heights.
    Bibliography: p.
    Includes index.
✓ 1. Brontë, Emily, 1818–1848.   Wuthering Heights.
✓ I. Title.
PR4172.W73H65 1985   823'.8⁰⁹ 85–5121
                        BRONTĒ, Ē.
ISBN 0–335–15087–X
ISBN 0–335–15073–X (pbk.)

Text design by Clarke Williams

Typeset by Marlborough Design
Printed in Great Britain by J. W. Arrowsmith Ltd, Bristol

For my mother, Doris Holderness

Contents

Series Editor's Preface

The intention of this series is to provide short introductory books about major writers, texts, and literary concepts for students of courses in Higher Education which substantially or wholly involve the study of Literature.

The series adopts a pedagogic approach and style similar to that of Open University material for Literature courses. *Open Guides* aim to inculcate the reading 'skills' which many introductory books in the field tend, mistakenly, to assume that the reader already possesses. They are, in this sense, 'teacherly' texts, planned and written in a manner which will develop in the reader the confidence to undertake further independent study of the topic. They are 'open' in two senses. First, they offer a three-way tutorial exchange between the writer of the *Guide*, the text or texts in question, and the reader. They invite readers to join in an exploratory discussion of texts, concentrating on their key aspects and on the main problems which readers, coming to the texts for the first time, are likely to encounter. The flow of a *Guide* 'discourse' is established by putting questions for the reader to follow up in a tentative and searching spirit, guided by the writer's comments, but not dominated by an over-arching and single-mindedly-pursued argument or evaluation, which itself requires to be 'read'.

Guides are also 'open' in a second sense. They assume that literary texts are 'plural', that there is no end to interpretation, and that it is for the reader to undertake the pleasurable task of discovering meaning and value in such texts. *Guides* seek to provide, in compact form, such relevant biographical, historical and cultural information as bears upon the reading of the text, and they point the reader to a selection of the best available critical discussions of it. They are not in themselves concerned to propose, or to counter, particular readings of the texts, but rather to put *Guide* readers in a position to do that for themselves. Experienced travellers learn to dispense with guides, and so it should be for readers of this series.

This *Open Guide* to Emily Bronte's *Wuthering Heights* is best studied in conjunction with the Penguin English Library text of the novel, edited by David Daiches (1965). Page references in the *Guide* are to this edition. Chapter references are also provided for the convenience of readers using a different edition.

Graham Martin

Acknowledgements

Earlier versions of this study guide benefited greatly from the help and criticism of Angus Calder, Cicely Havely, Arnold Kettle and John Purkis. In its present form it is indebted to Graham Martin, whose criticism and advice have shaped the book at every stage of writing.

Penny Windsor was kind enough to answer some queries about feminist criticism; Lee Poole and Alma La Grange handled the typing. Marilyn Partridge was, as always, a seminal and sustaining influence. Gratitude is also due to the students of the Swansea University Adult Education Department's Literature Foundation course, 1984–5 who provided the ideal forum for a testing of the book's methods and ideas.

My thanks go to the Open University for permission to develop this book from material originally contributed to their Twentieth Century Novel course.

1. Narrative

One writer, endowed with the keen vision and fine sympathies of genius, has discerned the real nature of *Wuthering Heights*, and has, with equal accuracy, noted its beauties and touched on its faults. Too often do reviewers remind us of the mob of Astrologers, Chaldeans and Soothsayers gathered before the 'writing on the wall', and unable to read the characters or make known the interpretation. We have a right to rejoice when a true seer comes at last . . . who can say with confidence, 'This is the interpretation thereof'.[1]

Whether it is right or advisable to create beings like Heathcliff, I do not know: I scarcely think it is. But this I know; the writer who possesses the creative gift owns something of which he is not always master – something that at times strangely wills and works for itself . . . Be the work grim or glorious, dread or divine, you have little choice left but quiescent adoption.[2]

When Charlotte Brontë wrote of the difficulty of her sister's novel, and the perplexity of its critics, she expressed the belief that a true and correct interpretation of the novel was in fact possible: and that one reviewer had approached, if not quite achieved, such a reading. In the second quoted passage, she expressed the opposite view: that the creative power of the artist is independent of even the author's conscious will, intellectual control and moral discipline. The reader's part is not to interpret but to submit, in passive obedience ('quiescent adoption') to that creative power.

Charlotte's terms and ideas are those of her age: but her observations draw attention to a contradiction still central to the practice of literary criticism. On the one hand we rest on the belief that a literary text has a true meaning, intrinsic to its artistic form, which could eventually be disclosed if we applied the correct methods of interpretation. On the other hand, we wouldn't expect any single reading or act of criticism to say the final word on a classic test, making all subsequent discussion useless. Much criticism proceeds by claiming the authority of a correct inter-

"Emily Brontë, by her brother Branwell (National Portrait Gallery)"

pretation, and apparently attempting to close the debate by disposing of all incorrect or irrelevant arguments. Yet criticism only remains possible if literature is conceived as 'open' rather than closed: a classic text is discussable because it continually offers itself to generation after generation of readers for 'reproduction', re-reading and re-interpretation, a question perpetually unanswered, a problem eternally unsolved.

In the past ten or fifteen years British literary criticism has undergone considerable change, partly as a result of the influence of French cultural theory, especially the methods of 'structuralism'. 'Post-structuralist' literary criticism holds that language is not a repository of meanings inherent in it, but raw material for the production of meaning: there is no fixed and final relationship between words and the meanings they signify; such relationships are changeable and subject to the determining influences of a society and its culture. In terms of such criticism *Wuthering Heights* is not the container of a fixed meaning, put into it by the author, to be withdrawn by readers equipped with the right 'key': it is rather a system of linguistic signs which produces many different meanings as it is read by different readers in different contexts. Frank Kermode, commenting on Charlotte Brontë's belief in the possibility of 'interpretation', observes that any reader looking up the review of Charlotte's 'true seer' would be disappointed; though in all probability no one would, since we instinctively reject the possibility of such finality of critical judgement, as strongly as we keep believing in its ultimate possibility:[3]

> It is in the nature of works of art to be open, in so far as they are 'good'; though it is in the nature of authors, and of readers, to close them.

The differences between traditional and post-structuralist approaches to *Wuthering Heights* are pursued further in Chapter Seven. I have raised the matter at the outset not only because it is important, but as a way of stressing that this *Guide* is not concerned to expound a 'correct', authoritative interpretation for the reader to follow. It aspires, as its title suggests, to be 'open' rather than closed in several different senses. It is not so much concerned to privilege one particular authoritative point of view (either my own or anyone else's), but rather to introduce you to something of the variety of available interpretations. These different views are not to be learned as a canon of privileged opinions: you too are, as a reader, a participant in this perpetual activity of making and re-making meaning from literary texts.

The *Guide* tries to be 'open' also to the presence of many different individual readers, engaged in the attempt to clarify and formalize *personal* experiences of the novel. You should be thinking of the *Guide* and the criticism it considers as raw material for the production of your own individual response to *Wuthering Heights*. The novel itself, if we handle it properly, will support this enterprise: the rich multiplicity of its artistic organization continually prompts the production of manifold meanings.

You will see as you work through the *Guide* what that means in practice. The *Guide* works partly by providing facts, raising questions, discussing issues: but its primary strategy is to assist your reading of the novel by referring you to sections of it, posing questions about the passages you read, then offering some organized 'discussion' of them. Don't think of this as a 'question and answer' exercise. The comments I provide under the sub-heading 'Discussion' are not model answers or prescriptive solutions: they may not resemble your discussion very closely, though the two should intersect in significant ways. You will not be learning from the *absorption* of my views, but from letting them *interact* with your own. You should aim therefore to produce in your 'discussion' notes, not the closest possible imitation of the ones provided here, but a version which, operating within the same framework, clarifies and formalizes your own personal and individual response to *Wuthering Heights*.

$$*\quad*\quad*\quad*\quad*\quad*\quad*\quad*\quad*$$

Let us begin by asking who tells this story, and how it is told.

> 1801. – I have just returned from a visit to my landlord – the solitary neighbour that I shall be troubled with. This is certainly a beautiful country! (Ch. 1, p. 45)

The speaker, Mr Lockwood, introduces us not only to Heathcliff and the strange world of Wuthering Heights, but directly to the issue of the novel's narrative technique. Narrative technique is, in the one sense, simply the method the novelist has chosen for telling a story: and in novels of this period, the main purpose of the method is usually to make the act of story-telling seem as real, as convincing and as natural as possible, by concentrating the reader's attention on the story, the characters, their history and their world. As we study a novel, examining its devices more closely, we come to realize that the chosen method of narration strongly influences our response to the imaginative 'world' the novel creates. If the story is told to us by a central character (first-person narrative), as in such novels as *Jane Eyre* or *David Copperfield*, the whole presentation tends to seem highly subjective: we experience one character's fate more intensively than that of any other. Or the story-teller can be an impersonal narrator, an authoritative voice speaking from outside the story, yet knowing all there is to know about it. The 'omniscient narrator' technique, as employed by Henry Fielding or George Eliot, confers a greater sense of *objectivity* on the telling of the story.

Wuthering Heights is like a modern *avant-garde* novel (and is for that reason peculiarly interesting to modern criticism) because its technique involves an emphasis on the devices of story-telling as well as on the telling of a story: the reader's attention is not concentrated wholly on the object of the narrative, but on the narrative itself and on the way in which the narrative constitutes its object, the story. *Wuthering Heights* has a peculiar narrative method, in which there is no first-person narrator, yet every word is spoken by a character in the story, and the author remains withdrawn: a method which combines the objectivity of impersonal narrative with the subjectivity of the first person. This method denies us any special intimacy with hero or heroine; nor do we have the reassuring authority of an impersonal narration. The novel is rather pervaded by a radical *uncertainty* about the story that is told. It displays a quality of ambiguity flowing not just from the presence of ghosts and mysteries, but from the absence of any reliable narrative *authority*. Where there is room for doubt about the accuracy of a witness' testimony, readers can hardly be positive in their convictions about what really 'happened'. The first word of the novel is 'I', suggesting the opening of a first-person narrative. But Mr Lockwood is *not* the novel's hero, and the substance of the story is not *his* experience. Nor does he transmit to us a clear understanding of the central character Heathcliff: in fact, his own reaction to Heathcliff is one of confused perplexity.

Let us examine Mr Lockwood's narrative more closely. Please read Chapters 1 and 2 of *Wuthering Heights*, paying particular attention to Lockwood's characterization of himself. Look carefully at the language. Underline the words and phrases that could be described as artificial, or cliché. What kind of man would you imagine talking like this?

While enjoying a month of fine weather at the sea-coast, I was
thrown into the company of a most fascinating creature, a real
goddess in my eyes, as long as she took no notice of me. I 'never told
my love' vocally; still, if looks have language, the merest idiot might
have guessed I was over head and ears: she understood me, at last,
and looked a return – the sweetest of all imaginable looks – and
what did I do? I confess it with shame – shrunk icily into myself, like
a snail, at every glance retired colder and farther; till, finally, the
poor innocent was led to doubt her own senses, and, overwhelmed
with confusion, persuaded her mamma to decamp. (Ch. 1, p. 48).

DISCUSSION

These are the phrases I have underlined: 'a most fascinating
creature'; 'a real goddess'; 'I never told my love'; 'over head and
ears'; 'persuaded her mamma to decamp'. The language is riddled
with clichés and conventional phrases; it suggests a superficial and
frivolous kind of man, perhaps a fashionable Regency dandy, or a
fairly ordinary kind of man affecting fashionable manners.

Lockwood reveals, by the language he uses, the *difference*
between himself and the people he is visiting. What about the
experience itself? He describes how he came close to a relationship
with a woman; but realizing that the connection was developing
beyond the level of flirtation, the social reflection of a relationship
without any real interchange of feeling, he bolted. Lockwood has
been confronted with the fact of passion, love, relationship, and he
has shrunk away from it. As you read the novel it will become clear
that Lockwood's shying away from passion is intended as a
contrast with the love of Catherine and Heathcliff. Later on, a
similar contrast is made between Heathcliff and Edgar Linton. Here
the contrast reinforces the differences between Lockwood and the
world of the Heights.

Lockwood then has retired into an affected misanthropist's
retreat in distant Yorkshire, pretending to isolate himself from
society like a Byronic hero brooding over a hidden sorrow. That's
how he sees himself, anyway. But he still remains the genteel city-
dweller, pleasantly companionable, anxious to be on friendly terms
with his neighbours. 'It is astonishing how sociable I feel myself
compared with him' (Ch. 1, p. 50). He can't understand why at the
Heights nobody utters 'a word of sociable conversation' (Ch. 2,
p. 56); and when nobody will admit him to the house he imagines
'perpetual isolation from your species' to be the worst possible kind
of punishment (Ch. 2, p. 51).

The meeting between Lockwood and Heathcliff is a collision

of two different and distinct social worlds: an independent, sociable city-dweller is introduced to a remote Yorkshire farmhouse where nothing is as he expects it to be. So naturally he begins to make mistakes. His first one is to mistake Heathcliff for what he himself is – an ordinary upper-class gentleman pretending to be a recluse, a dilettante misanthropist: 'I felt interested in a man who seemed more *exaggeratedly reserved* than myself' (Ch. 1, p. 45). 'Exaggeratedly reserved'– Lockwood implies that Heathcliff is putting it on, as he is himself, rather than demonstrating a *natural* reserve.

Lockwood proceeds to make a series of mistakes about the Heights and its people, each one getting him deeper and deeper into misapprehension. He compliments Cathy on her 'favourites', only to discover that they are dead rabbits. He assumes that Cathy will be as amiable and hospitable as the ladies of his own social milieu, but is swiftly disillusioned when she flings the teaspoon back into the caddy. He takes Hareton to be a servant or common labourer because of his dress and manner, and gets entirely the wrong idea about the system of relationships at the Heights.

Re-read Chapter 2 of the novel, noting what these pages tell us about Lockwood *and* about the people at Wuthering Heights. What do you think was Emily Brontë's purpose in arriving at her subject through the intermediary of Lockwood as a narrator of the first part of the story? Jot down a few notes on this question, and bear these in mind as you read the broader discussion on Emily Brontë's use of narrators, which follows here.

DISCUSSION

Lockwood narrates for the first three chapters. Then Nelly Dean, the servant alternately of the Earnshaws and the Lintons, becomes narrator for most of the novel: she transmits the story to Lockwood, who reports it in her own words, interposing sections of narrative in his own voice in Chapters 31 and 32, and at the novel's conclusion. Substantial passages of narrative from other characters appear in Catherine's diary (Chapter 3); Heathcliff's account of a visit to Thrushcross Grange (Chapter 6); Isabella Linton's letter to Nelly (Chapter 13) and the subsequent narrative of her life at the Heights (Chapter 17); and a section of narrative from the younger Catherine (Chapter 24). Shorter passages come from Catherine (Chapter 12), from Heathcliff (Chapter 29) and from the servant Zillah (Chapter 30). As you read the novel, notice the individual characters and voices of the different narrators, and the particular colouring they give to their versions of the same event.

The central question to bear in mind constantly, is why Emily Brontë should have chosen to use the technique of multiple narrative for her novel. Some critics have argued that the function of the two chief narrators, Lockwood and Nelly, is to reveal the inadequacy of empirical, commonsense judgement when confronted with mysterious or supernatural phenomena. When Nelly tries to explain away spiritual happenings, she is showing how little of experience she really understands. One critic has argued that

> Everything is contained in the mind of Lockwood, who begins the novel with his curious poking about the Heights ... trying to understand and interpret what he sees. Nelly is like Lockwood, both in her need to understand and in having staked her comprehension of life on the objective level of empirical reality. She lives in a world of things and of rational casual explanations of events: here she is secure, in control, and is being rewarded for her control. Anything not reducible to this level of existence is, for both Lockwood and Nelly, a threat to their hold on reality.[4]

But another attaches more value to the rationalism and 'normality' of Nelly Dean, proposing that it helps to keep the novel believable (though with the qualification that rationality is at least partly inadequate):

> The roles of the two narrators, Lockwood and Nelly Dean, are not casual. Their function (they are the two most 'normal' people in the book) is partly to keep the story close to the earth, to make it believable, partly to comment on it from a common-sense point of view and thereby to reveal in part the inadequacy of such common sense. They act as a kind of sieve to the story, sometimes a double sieve, which has the purpose not simply of separating off the chaff, but of making us aware of the difficulty of passing easy judgements.[5]

You may feel that this *identification* of Lockwood and Nelly will not do: are they not in fact very different characters, who offer different perspectives on what they see, articulated in different languages? I will be returning to that point in my Chapter 5: the important point made by both these critics is that each narrator is involved in an attempt to interpret – to analyse, evaluate, understand – the strange, unfamiliar, even mysterious events that take place in the novel. As readers we also are involved in that effort of interpretation, and the narrators – whether we see them as blind or perceptive, illuminating or misleading – can in some sense show us the way, by attaining insights we can endorse, or making errors we can detect.

I would like you now to make a detailed comparison between two passages of narrative, in which two different characters offer contrasting accounts of Heathcliff's behaviour. Please read Chapters 16 and 17 of *Wuthering Heights*. Then study and make notes on the following passages. The object of the exercise is to compare how Nelly and Isabella see Heathcliff. Chapters 16 and 17 contain very different descriptions of Heathcliff's behaviour in the same emotional crisis, immediately after the death of Catherine.

(a) He was there – at least a few yards further in the park: leant against an old ash tree, his hat off, and his hair soaked with the dew that had gathered on the budded branches, and fell pattering round him. He had been standing a long time in that position, for I saw a pair of ousels passing and repassing scarcely three feet from him, busy in building their nest, and regarding his proximity no more than that of a piece of timber. They flew off at my approach, and he raised his eyes and spoke:

'She's dead!' he said; 'I've not waited for you to learn that. Put your handkerchief away – don't snivel before me. Damn you all! She wants none of *your* tears!'

I was weeping as much for him as her: we do sometimes pity creatures that have none of the feeling either for themselves or others; and when I first looked into his face I perceived that he had got intelligence of the catastrophe; and a foolish notion struck me that his heart was quelled, and he prayed, because his lips moved, and his gaze was bent on the ground.

'Yes, she's dead!' I answered, checking my sobs and drying my cheeks. 'Gone to heaven, I hope, where we may, everyone, join her, if we take due warning, and leave our evil ways to follow good!'

'Did *she* take due warning, then?' asked Heathcliff, attempting a sneer. 'Did she die like a saint? Come, give me a true history of the event. How did – '

He endeavoured to pronounce the name, but could not manage it, and compressing his mouth he held a silent combat with his inward agony, defying, meanwhile, my sympathy with an unflinching, ferocious stare.

'How did she die?' he resumed, at last – fain, notwithstanding his hardihood, to have a support behind him, for, after the struggle, he trembled, in spite of himself, to his very fingerends.

'Poor wretch!' I thought, 'you have a heart and nerves the same as your brother men! Why should you be so anxious to conceal them? Your pride cannot blind God! You tempt Him to wring them, till He forces a cry of humiliation!'

...'May she wake in torment!' he cried, with frightful

vehemence, stamping his foot, and groaning in a sudden
paroxysm of ungovernable passion. . .

He dashed his head against the knotted trunk; and, lifting up
his eyes, howled, not like a man, but like a savage beast getting
goaded to death with knives and spears.   (Ch. 16, pp. 202–4)

(b) 'Heathcliff did not glance my way, and I gazed up and
contemplated his features almost as confidently as if they had
been turned to stone. His forehead, that I once thought so
manly, and that I now think so diabolical, was shaded with a
heavy cloud; his basilisk eyes were nearly quenched by
sleeplessness – and weeping, perhaps, for the lashes were wet
then: his lips devoid of their ferocious sneer, and sealed in an
expression of unspeakable sadness. Had it been another, I
would have covered my face, in the presence of such grief. In *his*
case, I was gratified: and ignoble as it seems to insult a fallen
enemy, I couldn't miss this chance of sticking in a dart; his
weakness was the only time when I could taste the delight of
paying wrong for wrong.'

'Fie, fie, Miss!' I interrupted. 'One might suppose you had
never opened a Bible in your life. If God afflict your enemies,
surely that ought to suffice you. It is both mean and
presumptuous to add your torture to his!'   (Ch. 17, p. 215)

DISCUSSION (a)

Nelly's feelings move and change during this passage. When she
first looks at Heathcliff he seems more like a natural object than a
human being. His hair is wet with dew; the birds don't notice him;
he looks like a piece of timber. This passage could be used to argue
that Heathcliff is more an elemental force or a nature-spirit, than a
human being. This is obviously what Nelly thinks too: as a piece of
timber Heathcliff *must* be hard, obdurate, unfeeling, and she
suspects that he is: 'we do sometimes pity creatures that have none
of that feeling either for themselves or for others' (Ch. 16, p. 203).

She detects signs in Heathcliff's face that he may be grieving
for Catherine, but thinks that at first a 'foolish notion'. But at last
Nelly realizes that the 'defiance' of sympathy, the assumed
hardness, does not indicate lack of emotion. Heathcliff is wrung to
the heart and is trying to control the feeling, to master it by his
apparent hardness. He isn't an unfeeling lump of wood, or an
anonymous natural energy; he is human, and therefore his feelings
are perfectly natural: 'Poor wretch! . . . You have a heart and
nerves the same as your brother men! Why should you be anxious
to conceal them?' (Ch. 16, p. 203). The exchange of feelings

between Heathcliff and Nelly – she offering sympathy, he refusing it and struggling to control his grief – is a human situation.

Certainly Heathcliff shatters it by his subsequent outburst: 'May she wake in torment!' We can understand his feelings as Nelly describes them, but this speech is obviously puzzling. Nelly now sees him as 'not like a man, but like a savage beast getting goaded to death with knives and spears' (Ch. 16, p. 203). Still the savagery is a response to something *outside* himself: Heathcliff is *'getting goaded'* to death by an external agency (the deliberate awkwardness of the expression emphasizes it). Catherine's rejection of him, her marriage to Edgar and her death are the forces which assail him: he is a passive victim of intolerable torture: hence his savagery. By using the image of the tortured animal Nelly is once again putting Heathcliff into a context where we can understand his reactions. We may be puzzled by his strange metaphysical speculations, but we recognize the cry of an animal in pain.

DISCUSSION (b)

Isabella comes to quite different conclusions about Heathcliff: her answer to her own question, 'Is Mr Heathcliff a man?' (Ch. 13, p. 173) is a decided negative. She sees him entirely in terms of the supernatural – his countenance is 'diabolical', his eyes like 'the clouded windows of hell' (Ch. 17, p. 217). Earlier she spoke of him as a 'monster' with a 'devilish nature' (Ch. 17, p. 209). Nelly challenges Isabella's account as blasphemous; and earlier in Chapter 17 insisted on Heathcliff's humanity: 'He's a human being! . . . There are worse men than he is yet!' (p. 209). This affirmation is consistent with Nelly's sympathetic vision of Heathcliff. Isabella denies his humanity, and seeks gratification in his suffering.

The conflict in Chapter 17 seems initiated by Isabella: her part in it is one of provocation and exasperation – she deliberately gets on Heathcliff's nerves: 'I experienced pleasure in being able to exasperate him' (p. 209). In that same paragraph we find another of the frequent passive constructions, so often applied to Heathcliff, which seem to suggest that he doesn't so much initiate violence as receive it – 'he *was worked up* to forget'. The calculated provocations culminate in Isabella's offering Heathcliff the really significant insult: '"If poor Catherine had trusted you, and assumed the ridiculous, contemptible, degrading title of Mrs Heathcliff, she would soon have presented a similar picture!"' (Ch. 17, p. 217). Isabella knows how to hurt Heathcliff. By playing upon the circumstances of Catherine's choice between Edgar and Heathcliff, reminding him that he was the loser because he had no wealth, property or status, she hits upon the very reasons why Heathcliff has her as a prisoner – to revenge himself against her brother and her class. Not surprisingly, Heathcliff hits back.

Here we have seen one narrator, who is herself inclined towards superstition, nevertheless concluding that Heathcliff's *emotions* (if not all his actions) are entirely explicable in terms of familiar human experiences: the inconsolable quality of his bereavement drives him to excesses of passionate grief. In contrast, the other narrator states explicitly that she can find in Heathcliff no human self capable of claiming compassion: she finds it necessary to call on a language of supernatural evil to express the truth about his personality.

These contrasting accounts were obviously juxtaposed for us to compare and evaluate. Which, if either, offers a truer, more authentic vision of Heathcliff? Perhaps Nelly's intuitive insight and sympathetic understanding take us to the heart of Heathcliff's suffering. On the other hand, perhaps her Christian piety and tolerant rationalism are an attempt to falsify Heathcliff's nature by taming and domesticating what is in reality terribly mysterious and irredeemably alien. Would we not find Heathcliff infinitely less interesting if he permitted Nelly's 'skill' to console him? Isabella's vision, on the other hand, freely acknowledges, perhaps even thrills to, the sense of something violently inhuman and powerfully malevolent. Perhaps her vision is based on a misconception, because of its externality: unlike Nelly, she doesn't know Heathcliff's history or the world of Wuthering Heights; and her initial attraction to him was to something not quite human – a 'hero of chivalric romance' (Ch. 14, p. 187). Is her account like Lockwood's, more an expression of the stranger's bewilderment than the well-informed witness' testimony? Or could it be that Isabella, instinctively attuned by a perverse sexual attraction to the violent and mysterious darkness of Heathcliff's nature, has a better insight into the destructive power of his passion, and the implacable cruelty of his revenge?

I leave the questions open because it seems to me that the important point is the presence in the same novel of *both* these narrative perspectives. It has already been pointed out that *Wuthering Heights* is remarkable for the particularly wide variety of critical interpretations it has attracted; and I have suggested that one possible reason for this may be the evident *plurality* of the text itself. The technique of multiple narrative may be concerned to insist on the irreducible complexity of reality, rather than to privilege one interpretation over another.

If you would like to pursue this argument about narrative to some additional examples, you could consider Heathcliff's account of Thrushcross Grange in Chapter 6 (pp. 88–92), which offers an inverted version of Lockwood's arrival at the Heights; or Chapter 32, where Lockwood and Joseph provide very different views of the changes at Wuthering Heights (Ch. 32, pp. 338–9); or at the closing pages of the novel, where the mystery of Heathcliff and Catherine's apparitions is commented on differently by four separate individuals.

2. Heathcliff

Heathcliff is really the central problem of *Wuthering Heights*: our valuation of him determines our sense of what the novel is about. If you think about it, it would perhaps be more orthodox to regard Edgar Linton – who has all the conventional requirements – as the hero, and Heathcliff as the villain of the piece. Heathcliff never does anything virtuous or noble in the conventional sense: his story is a long list of morally reprehensible actions. Are we supposed to see Heathcliff (in the words of the *Examiner*, 8 January 1848: see below p. 80) as 'an incarnation of evil qualities; implacable hate, ingratitude, falsehood, selfishness, and revenge' – and despise him? Or are we supposed to sympathize with him in his obsessive pursuit of love and then revenge?

In Section II of my Chapter 7, which deals with contemporary responses to the novel, you will read that in the 1840s critics were divided on the subject of the book's 'morality'. Those who thought the book *immoral* seem to have assumed that Emily Brontë wanted us to admire the obviously immoral Heathcliff. Those who thought it moral assumed that she wanted us to judge him. These two ways of looking at him aren't the only ones, but they are the most common. How then are we supposed to see Heathcliff?

If we look at what he actually does in the novel, in the abstract, it's a pretty disgusting performance. This process is attempted in a critical article by Philip Drew called 'Charlotte Brontë as a critic of *Wuthering Heights*'.[1] Drew thinks that Charlotte's judgement on Heathcliff was correct: 'Heathcliff . .·. never once swerving in his arrow-straight course to perdition'. (*Preface*, p.40). She solved the problem of orientation within the moral world of the novel – the problem of knowing what we should think, what we should feel, how we should value – by reading it firmly within a known and recognizable moral system. As Drew writes:

> Charlotte's assessment of Heathcliff depends on a recognition of his superhuman villainy, whereas modern critics . . . usually choose to minimise or justify Heathcliff's consistent delight in malice in order to elevate him to the status of a hero.

Drew then provides a long catalogue or charge-sheet of Heathcliff's actual misdemeanours. Catherine calls him 'a pitiless, wolvish man' (Ch. 10, p. 141), and this assessment, Drew argues, is borne out by his actions. When he returns to Wuthering Heights as an adult, he immediately begins to lead Hindley Earnshaw to perdition; he courts Isabella Linton not out of love but desire for revenge; he breaks up the marriage between Catherine and Edgar; he has a fight with Hindley in which he knocks him down and kicks him; there is evidence that he murders Hindley; he degrades and perverts Hareton; he treats his own son Linton with great cruelty, trapping the second Cathy into marrying him, and finally letting him die without calling a doctor. All these actions are perpetrated with a savage and voracious appetite for inflicting cruelty. Drew sums up:

> His whole career is one of calculated malice: during this time he does not perform one good or kindly action, and continually expresses his hatred of all other characters. So extreme is his malevolence that one might expect him to impress critics as a grotesque villain like Quilp in *The Old Curiosity Shop*.[1]

Some readers respond sympathetically to this hostile view of Heathcliff. Others feel that there is much more to admire both in Heathcliff's character and in what he represents: the figure of quenchless love, enormous suffering, irrepressible pride and resolute refusal to submit to circumstances or fate. Philip Drew's own critical approach should perhaps also be subjected to some interrogation: do we really respond to the actions of a fictional character in exactly the same way as we would to such actions performed by a real person? If Heathcliff does not impress readers as a grotesque villain like Quilp, does that not indicate some profound difference of artistic effect? You must of course reach your own decision about Heathcliff, as about every other aspect of the novel: to assist you I will offer two alternative ways of thinking about Heathcliff himself, before proceeding to consider him in relation to Catherine.

Please read Chapter 4 of *Wuthering Heights*, then study and make notes on the following passage, which desribes Heathcliff's initiation into Wuthering Heights and into the Earnshaw family. How is he regarded by the family, and how treated? Does Nelly's judgement that he 'bred bad feeling in the house' seem to you justified, or adequate?

They entirely refused to have it in bed with them, or even in their room, and I had no more sense, so I put it on the landing of the stairs, hoping it might be gone on the morrow. By chance, or else attracted by hearing his voice, it crept to Mr Earnshaw's door and there he found it on quitting his chamber. Inquiries were made as to how it got there; I was obliged to confess, and in recompense for my cowardice and inhumanity was sent out of the house.

This was Heathcliff's first introduction to the family: on coming back a few days afterwards, for I did not consider my banishment perpetual, I found that they had christened him 'Heathcliff'; it was the name of a son who died in childhood, and it has served him ever since, both for Christian and surname.

Miss Cathy and he were now very thick; but Hindley hated him, and to say the truth I did the same; and we plagued and went on with him shamefully, for I wasn't reasonable enough to feel my injustice, and the mistress never put in a word on his behalf, when she saw him wronged.

He seemed a sullen, patient child; hardened, perhaps to ill-treatment: he would stand Hindley's blows without winking or shedding a tear, and my pinches moved him only to draw in a breath and open his eyes, as if he had hurt himself by accident and nobody was to blame. This endurance made old Earnshaw furious when he discovered his son persecuting the poor, fatherless child, as he called him. He took to Heathcliff strangely, believing all he said (for that matter, he said precious little, and generally the truth), and petting him up far above Cathy, who was too mischievous and wayward for a favourite.

So, from the very beginning, he bred bad feeling in the house; and at Mrs Earnshaw's death, which happened in less than two years after, the young master had learnt to regard his father as an oppressor rather than a friend, and Heathcliff as a usurper of his parent's affections and his privileges, and he grew bitter with brooding over these injuries. (Ch. 4, pp. 78–9)

DISCUSSION

The most striking aspect of the family's reaction to Heathcliff is its immediate and instinctive hostility. Nelly consistently refers to the child as 'it', denying Heathcliff any human status. He is not only treated with callous indifference, he is subjected to active and gratuitous cruelty. Consider the succession of verbs denoting ill-treatment in the three paragraphs beginning 'Miss Cathy and he were now very thick' – *hated, plagued, wronged, hardened, persecuting*; all summed up in the single word *injustice*.

The 'bad feeling' Heathcliff arouses seems entirely disproportionate to what he is and does. Is it that this close-knit family structure, with its long ancestral past, is threatened and challenged by the arrival of an outsider, a stranger who has no proper place in the family? One who simply requires acceptance, without claim or justification? Evidently the 'bad feeling' arises from within the family itself, rather than from Heathcliff.

The 'gipsy brat' old Mr Earnshaw brings home with him has neither name nor status, property nor possessions. He emerges from that darkness which is the *outside* of the tightly-knit family system: an outsider who *tests* the family by introducing an alien element into a jealously-guarded system of parental and filial relations, of inheritance and possession. 'You must e'en take it as a gift from God', says old Mr Earnshaw 'though it's as dark as if it came from the devil' (Ch. 4, p. 77). Heathcliff can be either gift or threat, by virtue of his single passive demand, to be loved: Catherine takes the opportunity of loving him, and thereby disturbs the family's equilibrium. Hindley sees Heathcliff as a rival for his father's affections and his own position as heir, a potential disrupter of the ancient lineage; and accordingly hates him. Heathcliff here is not the instigator but the recipient of violence: violence which his arrival has provoked in that defensive, exclusive family unit. The violence, then, is latent in the family structure, and provoked by an individual who expects to be treated as an equal.

Naturally, however, these experiences have their effect on him: we begin to see emerging a representative pattern of victimization begetting violence, injustice provoking resentment. Heathcliff doesn't remain a victim all his life: he deliberately resolves to free himself from the humiliation of oppression by attaining for himself the status of an oppressor. His plan of revenge, carefully laid and executed, is to revenge himself on Hindley and the Lintons by two methods: oppressing and exploiting their children, Hareton and Linton Heathcliff, in precisely the same way that Hindley and

Edgar oppressed and exploited Heathcliff; and by expropriating their lands and possessions and seizing them himself. Heathcliff makes the identification between himself and Hareton very clear:

'Now, my bonny lad, you are *mine*! And we'll see if one tree won't grow as crooked as another, with the same wind to twist it!' (Ch. 17, p. 222)

I think most readers find it difficult to sympathize with Heathcliff's actions after he returns, even though we may recognize in them a 'rough moral justice'. It would surely be impossible to sympathize wholly with him, since our initial sympathy went to him as a victim of oppression – and we very soon see that in order to secure his revenge he has become an oppressor himself:

'The tyrant grinds down his slaves – and they don't turn against him, they crush those beneath them. You are welcome to torture me to death for your amusement, only, allow me to amuse myself a little in the same style – And refrain from insult as much as you are able. Having levelled my palace, don't erect a hovel and complacently admire your own charity in giving me that for a home'. (Ch. 11, p. 151)

But if Heathcliff, the novel's only candidate for the status of 'hero', loses our sympathy in respect of his actions, where does it go? Do we begin to take sides with the Lintons, or is a vacuum of sympathy set up in the novel? For the answer to this question I'd like you to read the beginning of Chapter 11 up to 'Heathcliff had promised that!' (pp. 147–9).

DISCUSSION

Doesn't the movement of feeling here seem to indicate the direction the novel is taking? In Chapter 10 Nelly conceives an intense dislike for Heathcliff. At the beginning of Chapter 11 the direction of her feelings guides our own – towards the child Hareton, who is now in the position Heathcliff occupied formerly. Hindley and Hareton are now victims of a tyrant: we feel sympathy for them, not the tyrant himself.

Hareton develops from this point into a very important element in the novel. The development of the relationship between him and Cathy is a continuation of the Catherine–Heathcliff relationship. Please study and make notes on the following passage. Why does Heathcliff avoid striking Cathy?

He had his hand in her hair; Hareton attempted to release the locks, entreating him not to hurt her that once. His black eyes flashed, he seemed ready to tear Catherine in pieces, and I was just worked up to risk coming to the rescue, when of a sudden his fingers relaxed, he shifted his grasp from her head to her arm, and gazed intently in her face – Then, he drew his hand over his eyes, stood a moment to collect himself apparently, and turning anew to Catherine, said with assumed calmness, 'You must learn to avoid putting me in a passion, or I shall really murder you, some time!' (Ch. 33, p. 350)

DISCUSSION

Because, seeing Hareton and Cathy unite in love and comradeship against brutal and tyrannical oppression, he recognizes himself and Catherine as they were together, rebelling against an oppressive regime. Heathcliff has come to see the emptiness of his triumph: he has recognized that Hareton is himself; Catherine's daughter, Catherine. He has achieved the same moral insight into them as we have into Heathcliff himself in the early stages of the novel.

So far in this discussion of Heathcliff we have been considering the characters and events *naturalistically*: that is, in terms of the predictable cause-and-effect relationships, the familiar patterns of probability and consequence which seem generally to hold in our ordinary everyday lives. The image of a child becoming brutalized as a consequence of sustained and systematic ill-treatment is not something that happens only in books. On the other hand, there are in the novel incidents and states of mind which seem to defy such naturalistic explanation: a ghost appearing at a bedroom window, even if we were inclined to credit such a possibility, is not an *ordinary* experience. We could perhaps relate some of Heathcliff's behaviour (such as his proposal to pervert Hareton to revenge his own perversion) to familiar dimensions of experience. But when he tells Nelly of his attempt to disinter Catherine's corpse (Chapter 29), we are transported into another dimension, one of bizarre and mysterious happenings, intense and extreme sensations, incredible and outlandish practices.

There is nothing at all unusual or surprising in this capacity of literature to mingle reality and fantasy, fact and fiction. Provided that the work of art we are experiencing operates consistently within its chosen 'convention', whether that be realism or fantasy, we are not disturbed: but if an extra-terrestrial alien walked onto the set of *Coronation Street*, or a character from *Coronation Street* appeared in a science-fiction film, we would find the effect dislocating – perhaps humorous and appropriate, perhaps ludicrous and unsatisfying. *Wuthering Heights* is the kind of novel that operates with different conventions: working at times with the

probability and familiarity of realism, at times with the supernatural and fantastic.

Chapter 6 of this *Guide* contains a full discussion of these
aspects of the novel: for the moment I would like you to think of
Heathcliff in terms of some of the non-realistic conventions Emily
Brontë employs.

Please read Chapter 29 of the novel, then study the following
passage and make notes on it. In what sort of context would you
expect to encounter a scene such as this? What explanation can you
give of Heathcliff's action and emotions?

'I'll tell you what I did yesterday! I got the sexton, who was digging
Linton's grave, to remove the earth off her coffin lid, and I opened it.
I thought, once, I would have stayed there, when I saw her face
again – it is hers yet – he had hard work to stir me; but he said it
would change, if the air blew on it, and so I struck one side of the
coffin loose – and covered it up – not Linton's side, damn him! I
wish he'd been soldered in lead – and I bribed the sexton to pull it
away, when I'm laid there, and slide mine out too – I'll have it made
so, and then, by the time Linton gets to us, he'll not know which is
which!'

'You were very wicked, Mr Heathcliff!' I exclaimed; 'were you not
ashamed to disturb the dead?'

'I disturbed nobody, Nelly,' he replied; 'and I gave some ease to
myself. I shall be a great deal more comfortable now; and you'll have
a better chance of keeping me underground, when I get there.
Disturbed her? No! she has disturbed me, night and day, through
eighteen years – incessantly – remorselessly – till yesternight – and
yesternight, I was tranquil. I dreamt I was sleeping the last sleep, by
that sleeper, with my heart stopped, and my cheek frozen against
hers . . .

'The day she was buried there came a fall of snow. In the evening I
went to the churchyard. It blew bleak as winter – all round was
solitary: I didn't fear that her fool of a husband would wander up the
den so late – and no one else had business to bring them there.

'Being alone, and conscious two yards of loose earth was the sole
barrier between us, I said to myself –

'"I'll have her in my arms again! If she be cold, I'll think it is
this north wind that chills me; and if she be motionless, it is sleep."

'I got a spade from the toolhouse, and began to delve with all my
might – it scraped the coffin; I fell to work with my hands; the wood
commenced cracking about the screws, I was on the point of
attaining my object, when it seemed that I heard a sigh from some
one above, close at the edge of the grave, and bending down. "If I
can only get this off," I muttered, "I wish they may shovel in the
earth over us both!" and I wrenched more desperately still. There
was another sigh, close at my ear. I appeared to feel the warm breath
of it displacing the sleet-laden wind. I knew no living thing in flesh

and blood was by – but as certainly as you perceive the approach to some substantial body in the dark, though it cannot be discerned, so certainly I felt that Cathy was there, not under me, but on the earth. (Ch. 29, pp. 319–21)

DISCUSSION

The whole account (for here Heathcliff himself is narrator) seems to belong to a horror-story, a tale of mystery and imagination. Heathcliff acts like a body-snatcher, or a necrophiliac lover, or even the 'ghoul or vampire' Nelly sometimes suspects him to be (Chapter 34): he even anticipates having problems in staying underground after his own death. His passion for Catherine acknowledges no limitation, not even the separation of death: his desire for her seems here almost necrophiliac, as he imagines sleeping with her in the grave, their corpses dissolving into each other in an eternity of horrifying physical sensuality.

Wuthering Heights draws to some extent on the contemporary equivalent of the horror story, the Gothic romance: and in the light of this passage it is not surprising to learn that one direct source of the novel was a tale of passion and mystery published in *Blackwood's Magazine* (November 1840), called *The Bridegroom of Barna*,[2] a fairly typical example of popular 'Gothic' fiction. Its hero, Hugh Lawlor, represents the popular convention of the Byronic hero – the figure of the dark, mysterious and melancholy exile which found its fullest expression in the poems of Byron (for example *The Giaour, The Corsair, Childe Harold*), and flourished in nineteenth-century romances and tales of the Gothic tradition. The Byronic hero was usually a wanderer, exiled from his native land, bearing the burden of some enormously wicked but nameless and mysterious crime, and frequently distinguished by the physical type of dark good looks conferred on the tradition by Byron himself. The figure is an early example of what we now familiarly call an 'anti-hero': though he is a rebel, a criminal, a transgressor of moral codes and social conventions, he is still often the author's 'hero' – he has the author's sympathy and he bears the book's positive values. The figure compelled the imagination strongly in the Romantic period: it evidently embodied an important experience of alienation, self-conscious separation from social norms, rejection of moral and social convention.

Hugh Lawlor in *The Bridegroom of Barna* has all the characteristics of the dark hero – a noble origin and a fundamentally noble nature, a flashing eye and a terrifying stare, and the consciousness of an enormous guilt: 'like the first murderer, a fugitive upon the earth, with a curse as deep as Cain's pursuing his footsteps' (p. 698). Hugh's crime is a murder which he has committed on behalf of the girl he loves, Ellen Nugent: 'to his lonely and affectionate spirit, Ellen was all the world – the only living thing that he felt necessary to his existence' (p. 697). Ellen dies of consumption, and Hugh goes on the run. He is finally apprehended in the churchyard where his lover was buried; he has disinterred her and sits by the grave embracing her corpse. He is killed on the spot, and the two bodies buried together: 'the strangers who dug his grave did not venture to separate in death the hapless pair who in life could never be united' (p. 704).

The Bridegroom of Barna is a melodrama typical of the popular fiction it belongs to, and Emily Brontë transformed its devices into a much more complex and interesting fictional method. In *Wuthering Heights* 'Gothic' conventions are not used for their own sake, for the sensational *frisson* available from contemplation of 'taboo' subjects such as incest or necrophilia. They are used, we might say, to express and describe a very extreme and peculiar state of mind and feeling. Heathcliff's desire to see and embrace Catherine's corpse is not, the context of the novel tells us, a simple 'case' of necrophilia: it is an illustration of the nature of Heathcliff's passion, its refusal to accept any limitations, even those imposed by death and burial. His wish to be buried with Catherine is not a gratuitous touch of sensationalism but a simple translation of romantic 'merging' into physical terms. While Catherine speaks of their love as an infinite spiritual bond, it is characteristic of Heathcliff to give physical substance to Catherine's metaphysical affirmation. Heathcliff's feeling that Catherine's presence is near him as he ransacks the grave, is for him an encounter with her ghost ('I have a strong faith in ghosts') (Ch. 29, p. 320); but his desperate pursuit of an elusive phantom, his obsessive conviction of the presence of the dead, is surely a human – indeed, a common – response to bereavement.

We could conclude that material from a particular type of literature is offered in *Wuthering Heights*, not in a simple and unselfconscious way, but in a way that enriches and complicates the conventional forms. Where the Gothic style uses such material simply because it is extreme, for the fascination of its extremity, *Wuthering Heights* uses it to describe and express an extreme state of mind and feeling, which we can find fascinating and even awe-inspiring, but which can also be understood. The 'horror story' material, for all its strangeness, at once distances Heathcliff and brings him closer to us, bringing wonder and fear at that which is within us all.

3. The Lovers

Though Heathcliff is clearly an arresting and memorable figure in
his own right, he cannot adequately be considered in isolation from
his relationship with Catherine. I propose to introduce a number of
approaches to that relationship, first by dwelling on certain
passages from the earlier chapters of the novel, then by alerting you
to some of the current critical viewpoints. The three incidents to be
discussed are the account in Catherine's diary of the 'awful Sunday'
(Chapter 3); the visit of the two children to Thrushcross Grange
(Chapter 6); and Catherine's declaration to Nelly of her love for
Heathcliff (Chapter 9). In each case I will make some brief
comments on the passage, suggesting how you might deal with it as
a piece of writing. At the same time I will be posing questions
intended to develop your own sense of the meaning of a particular
passage; and to bring to bear on the novel the arguments which you
will have to examine, compare and evaluate for yourself.

'An awful Sunday'

Please read Chapter 3 of the novel, then study the following passage
and make notes on it. What is your *valuation* of the actions of
Catherine and Heathcliff? Do you see them simply as naughty
children, defying their elders, disrupting the order of the house-
hold?

> 'An awful Sunday!' commenced the paragraph beneath. 'I wish my
> father were back again. Hindley is a detestable substitute – his
> conduct to Heathcliff is atrocious – H. and I are going to rebel – we
> took our initiatory step this evening.
>
> 'All day had been flooding with rain; we could not go to church,
> so Joseph must needs get up a congregation in the garret; and, while
> Hindley and his wife basked down stairs before a comfortable

fire – doing anything but reading their Bibles, I'll answer for it – Heathcliff, myself, and the unhappy plough-boy, were commanded to take our Prayer-books, and mount – we were ranged in a row, on a sack of corn, groaning and shivering, and hoping that Joseph would shiver too, so that he might give us a short homily for his own sake. A vain idea! The service lasted precisely three hours; and yet my brother had the face to exclaim, when he saw us descending,

'"What, done already?"

'On Sunday evenings we used to be permitted to play, if we did not make much noise; now a mere titter is sufficient to send us into corners!

'"You forget you have a master here," says the tyrant. "I'll demolish the first who puts me out of temper! I insist on perfect sobriety and silence. Oh, boy! was that you? Frances, darling, pull his hair as you go by; I heard him snap his fingers."

'Frances pulled his hair heartily, and then went and seated herself on her husband's knee; and there they were, like two babies, kissing and talking nonsense by the hour – foolish palaver that we should be ashamed of.

'We made ourselves as snug as our means allowed in the arch of the dresser. I had just fastened our pinafores together, and hung them up for a curtain, when in comes Joseph, on an errand from the stables. He tears down my handywork, boxes my ears, and croaks:

'"T'maister nobbut just buried, and Sabbath nut o'ered, und t' sahnd uh t' gospel still i' yer lugs, and yah dar be laiking! shame on ye! sit ye dahn, ill childer! they's good books eneugh if ye'll read 'em; sit ye dahn, and think uh yer sowls!"

'Saying this, he compelled us so to square our positions that we might receive, from the far-off fire, a dull ray to show us the text of the lumber he thrust upon us.

'I could not bear the employment. I took my dingy volume by the scroop, and hurled it into the dog-kennel, vowing I hated a good book.

'Heathcliff kicked his to the same place.

'Then there was a hubbub! (Ch. 3, pp. 62–3)

DISCUSSION

Catherine's diary describes the nature and quality of her early relationship with Heathcliff. When these events occur old Earnshaw is dead and Hindley is master of the Heights. We have seen already his policy of persecuting Heathcliff; in this account Catherine and Heathcliff are persecuted together – compelled to sit shivering in a garret, listening to Joseph reading sermons, while Hindley and his wife 'basked down stairs before a comfortable fire' (Ch. 3, p. 62). Their response to these conditions is to rebel against their repression.

Here are three possible interpretations, which I should like you to test against your own reactions. One point of view is that represented by Arnold Kettle in his *Introduction to the English Novel*. He thinks that we are introduced to the love of Catherine and Heathcliff as an emotional bond forged in response to their ill-treatment. Hindley's reaction to this show of resistance is to try to divide Catherine and Heathcliff by discriminating against the latter on grounds of class. Hindley 'swears he will reduce him to his right place' (Ch. 3, p. 64).

> Against this degradation Catherine and Heathcliff rebel, hurling their pious books into the dog-kennel. And in their revolt they discover their deep and passionate need of each other. He, the outcast slummy, turns to the lively, spirited, fearless girl who alone offers him understanding and comradeship. And she, born into the world of Wuthering Heights, senses that to achieve a full humanity, to be true to herself as a human being she must associate herself totally with him in his rebellion against the tyranny of the Earnshaws and all that tyranny involves.[1]

Now consider this passage from an essay by Dorothy van Ghent, 'On *Wuthering Heights*', from her book *The English Novel, Form and Function*:

> *Wuthering Heights* exists for the mind as a tension between two kinds of reality: the raw, inhuman reality of anonymous natural energies; and the restrictive reality of civilized habits, manners and codes. The first kind of reality is given to the imagination in the violent figures of Catherine and Heathcliff, portions of the flux of nature, children of rock and heath and tempest, striving to identify themselves as human, but disrupting all around them with their monstrous appetite for an inhuman kind of intercourse and finally disintegrated from within by the very energies out of which they are made.[2]

Dorothy van Ghent's approach doesn't see Catherine and Heathcliff responding violently to aggressive conditions, but as *naturally* and *spontaneously* anarchic and rebellious because they represent the destructive violence and amoral excess of uncivilized unconscious instinct. The bullying of Hindley and the fierce evangelical zeal of Joseph represent the 'restrictive reality of civilized habits, manners and codes', which attempt to contain the wild natural energy of the unregenerate unconscious.

These two critics thus attach quite different values to the same action. Writing more recently, a third critic has attempted to acknowledge both the 'social' and the 'metaphysical' dimensions of *Wuthering Heights*. Terry Eagleton in *Myths of Power*, like Arnold Kettle, sees history as the basis of the novel's fictional

"This illustration (and overleaf): Haworth and the surrounding countryside"

conflicts: but like Dorothy van Ghent he emphasizes that the novel expresses those conflicts in language and imagery that often point beyond society, beyond history itself.

> What Heathcliff offers Cathy is a non- or pre-social relationship, as the only authentic form of living in a world of exploitation and inequality, a world where one must refuse to measure oneself by the criteria of the class structure and so must appear inevitably subversive. Whereas in Charlotte's novels the love relationship takes you into society, in *Wuthering Heights* it drives you out of it. The love between Heathcliff and Catherine is an intuitive intimacy raised to cosmic status, by-passing the mediation of the 'social'; and this, indeed, is both its strength and its limit. Its non-sociality is on the one hand a revolutiionary refusal of the given language of social roles and values; and if the relationship is to remain unabsorbed by society it must therefore appear as natural rather than social, since Nature is the 'outside' of society. On the other hand, the novel cannot realize the meaning of that revolutionary refusal in social terms; the most it can do is to *universalize* that meaning by intimating the mysteriously impersonal energies from which the relationship springs.[3]

You will perhaps have noticed that none of these examples of critical practice is free from its own preconceptions and assumptions; in fact, each one is based on an underlying philosophy. Your reaction to a piece of criticism will inevitably involve in some way your attitude towards its philosophy. Dorothy van Ghent's essay, for example, is based on Freudian theory – she explicitly refers at the end of the quoted passage to Freud's theory of the 'death-wish'. Arnold Kettle's point of view is that of Marxist humanism; for him rebellion against oppression has a quite different, primarily social significance. Terry Eagleton's work is an attempt to fuse Marxism, psychoanalysis and post-structuralist literary criticism. Much criticism proceeds as if it did not have a philosophy at all, but were purely a neutral, spontaneous response to the objective qualities of a literary work. To use criticism effectively we need to be aware of its ideological basis. This shouldn't be taken to mean that we can only value criticism which shares our own opinions: if that were the case, criticism would always be telling us what we already know. Good criticism can reveal, illuminate, surprise and enlighten, whatever its ideology. And the variety of possible interpretations is a testimony to the nature of what we call 'literature', which can survive only if it contains that potentiality for meaningful reinterpretation by successive generations.

Of the three outlined views on this passage, I would say that the first and third carry a lot more weight. Catherine and Heathcliff are breaking up the order of what we take to be a fairly common

Victorian setting – where the parental authorities have absolute power to compel the children to do what they wish; where the children are made to suffer discomfort and privation for the good of their souls, and are offered as consolation the grim and gloomy Puritan Christianity of Joseph's sermon.

The actions of the two children, in first of all trying to make the best of the situation ('we made ourselves as snug as means allowed', Ch. 3, p. 63), and then, when this is taken from them, openly rebelling against Hindley's authority, are actions that can be condemned as inhuman only from the point of view of a Hindley or a Joseph. The rebellion is a rebellion that involves and implies alternative values. It isn't because they are non-human that they rebel; but precisely because they are fully human. They reject the order that deprives them of their humanity. Rebellion against society can be described as 'excess' only if we believe that the 'normality' of that society is completely fulfilling and completely human. In this case, it is obviously the reverse.

Which of these critical accounts do you find most persuasive? Can you assent to van Ghent's account of the childrens' rebellion? Do you feel the other two critics are justified in attributing a predominantly social meaning to the passage? Which critic seems to you to capture most precisely the form used by the novel to articulate its conflicts?

The two houses

The contrast and relationship between the two houses, the Heights and the Grange, is one of the basic thematic and structural techniques of the novel. As with every other aspect of *Wuthering Heights*, this conflict has been interpreted in various different ways. Clearly there is some kind of *social* difference between the two houses, though this has to be defined rather precisely. Both the Earnshaw and the Linton families belong to the class of the gentry; the families are at least socially compatible, if not of equal status. The marriage of Catherine and Edgar shows the two houses entering into some kind of alliance, excluding only the outsider Heathcliff, who has no rightful place in either. And yet there are strong differences of tone and atmosphere, of custom and convention – in short, of *culture* – which separate the two houses widely. The Earnshaw family is closer to the land and to agricultural labour; they could be described as a yeoman-farming family. The Linton house stands in a park, surrounded by a wall, a frontier between civilization and wild nature. The Heights has all the primitive roughness of a peasant life-style; the Grange the civilized luxury of an aristocratic society.

Please read Chapter 6 of the novel; considering and making notes on the following questions:

(a) In Chapter 6, Heathcliff is narrator of the description that introduces us to Thrushcross Grange. How would the description differ if Lockwood narrated it? How does the narrative technique direct our attention?

(b) Why is Heathcliff thrown out of the Grange and Catherine accepted?

(c) Heathcliff thinks Catherine will probably want to escape. She doesn't. What do you make of this?

DISCUSSION

(a) It's a very important narrative device that introduces us to Thrushcross Grange *from outside* rather than from inside. Imagine that Lockwood had narrated this passage instead of Heathcliff: the Grange to him would be normality, home. It is to Heathcliff as alien as the Heights was to Lockwood. Heathcliff recognizes in the Grange a potential heaven; but says that he wouldn't want to live there at any price. We can scarcely imagine the naive Lockwood looking at the Grange with such sardonic and contemptuous humour as Heathcliff does.

In the description of what they see through the window Heathcliff achieves an immediate and accurate perception of the nature of the Grange. He sees simultaneously the richness, splendour and luxury of the house, and the pettiness, triviality, nervous boredom and irritation of the children's lives. This is how one critic, Derek Traversi, analyses the impact of that description:

> The emphasis laid upon the soft and clinging luxury in which the Lintons live, protected by bulldogs and obsequious servants from the intrusion of the inferior world outside, is deliberately calculated to produce an impression of excessive sweetness and decay . . . The sight of so much unsuspected luxury certainly strikes the two children outside as 'beautiful'; but it also, more subtly, rouses in them a feeling of repudiation which is only intensified by the behaviour of the dwellers in this 'paradise'. The 'gold', the crimson carpets and chair-coverings which seem to deaden, to mollify the impact of life, the slightly unreal prettiness of the 'shower of glass drops hanging in silver chains', and the sense of barely-defined exquisite decadence in the reference to the little 'soft tapers': all these, seen through the eyes of the children outside, point to a highly significant contrast.[4]

(Incidentally it's worth observing that Isabella Linton displays the same childish, provoking, irritating nature in her later 'exasperation' of Heathcliff.)

Heathcliff claims that he wouldn't exchange his condition for Edgar Linton's at the Grange, and I think we feel that his judgement is correct. We have seen at the Heights – rough as it is – more humanity than there appears to be at the Grange. This is what I mean by the narrative technique directing our attention: encouraging us to value and judge what we see.

Heathcliff's assertion that he would have nothing to do with the kind of 'heaven' he sees in Thrushcross Grange is one of a pattern of metphors repeated in these early chapters. In Catherine's diary account of the 'awful Sunday' Hindley sits in a 'paradise on the hearth' (Ch. 3, p. 63); and when Catherine tells Nelly her dream she declares that she dreamt of going to the real heaven, and found it not to her liking: 'heaven did not seem to be my home; and I broke my heart with weeping to come back to earth . . . ' (Ch. 9, p. 120). The two children prefer their own would – in the arch of the dresser, or outside Thrushcross Grange – to the conventionally accepted paradise of genteel comfort and complacency. And when Catherine in her dream goes to the actual conventional heaven (which is probably quite like Thrushcross Grange) she wants to come back to Wuthering Heights.

(b)   The Lintons make a social distinction between Catherine and Heathcliff: 'she was a young lady; and they made a distinction between her treatment and mine' (Ch. 6, p. 92). The Lintons react to the invasion from outside with the instincts of property-owners: the children are assumed to be 'robbers', 'thieves', 'rascals' (pp. 90–1); guns and dogs are needed to protect the Lintons against their enemies. They light upon Heathcliff as an obvious candidate for the gallows – 'the villain scowls so plainly in his face, would it not be a kindness to the country to hang him at once, before he shows his nature in acts as well as features' (Ch. 6, p. 91). Mrs. Linton soon recognizes that he isn't in fact an old lag or hardened criminal; to her he is just 'a wicked boy, quite unfit for a decent house'. Heathcliff is 'placed': while Catherine is the daughter of a local landowner, he is a gipsy, a vagabond, a potential thief.

(c)   Heathcliff's corrosive narrative lays bare the real nature of the Grange, but he gravely underestimates its power. When he looks through the window he can see the Lintons being influenced by Catherine's energy and vitality. But he doesn't dream that there can be anything there strong enough to change Catherine. He is wrong. That distinction between Catherine and Heathcliff, their separation by class-distinction, and her seduction by the glamour of the Grange, are the beginning of Heathcliff's tragedy.

Please study and make notes on the following passage from Chapter 7. What kind of change has taken place in Catherine? How does the reader react to that change? What light does the passage throw on the contrast between the two houses?

Cathy stayed at Thrushcross Grange five weeks, till Christmas. By that time her ankle was thoroughly cured, and her manners much improved. The mistress visited her often, in the interval, and commenced her plan of reform by trying to raise her self-respect with fine clothes and flattery, which she took readily: so that, instead of a wild, hatless little savage jumping into the house, and rushing to squeeze us all breathless, there lighted from a handsome black pony a very dignified person, with brown ringlets falling from the cover of a feathered beaver, and a long cloth habit which she was obliged to hold up with both hands that she might sail in.

Hindley lifted her from her horse, exclaiming delightedly, 'Why, Cathy, you are quite a beauty! I should scarcely have known you – you look like a lady now – Isabella Linton is not to be compared with her, is she Frances?' . . .

'Is Heathcliff not here?' she demanded, pulling off her gloves, and displaying fingers wonderfully whitened with doing nothing, and staying in doors.

'Heathcliff, you may come forward' cried Mr Hindley, enjoying his discomfiture and gratified to see what a forbidding young blackguard he would be compelled to present himself. 'You may come in and wish Miss Catherine welcome, like the other servants.'

Cathy, catching a glimpse of her friend in his concealment, flew to embrace him; she bestowed seven or eight kisses on his cheek within the second, and then stopped, and drawing back, burst into a laugh, exclaiming,

'Why, how very black and cross you look! and how – how funny and grim! But that's because I'm used to Edgar and Isabella Linton. Well, Heathcliff, have you forgotten me?'

She had some reason to put the question, for shame and pride threw double gloom over his countenance, and kept him immoveable.

'Shake hands, Heathcliff,' said Mr Earnshaw, condescendingly; 'once in a way, that is permitted.'

'I shall not!' replied the boy, finding his tongue at last, 'I shall not stand to be laughed at, I shall not bear it!'

And he would have broken from the circle, but Miss Cathy seized him again.

'I did not mean to laugh at you,' she said, 'I could not hinder myself. Heathcliff, shake hands, at least! What are you sulky for? It was only that you looked odd – If you wash your face and brush your hair, it will be all right. But you are so dirty!'

She gazed concernedly at the dusky fingers she held in her own, and also at her dress, which she feared had gained no embellishment from its contact with his.

'You neen't have touched me!' he answered, following her eye and snatching away his hand. 'I shall be as dirty as I please, and I like to be dirty, and I will be dirty.' (Ch. 7, pp. 93–5).

DISCUSSION

Catherine returns from her stay at the Grange very much altered, from a 'hatless little savage' to 'a very dignified person' (Ch. 7, p. 93). It has been suggested that the nature of this change is a transformation of Catherine from a child to an adult:

> Cathy's narrative ends with her plans for a scamper on the moor in the rain, beneath the dairy woman's cloak. It is not until Heathcliff's account of that night's scamper that we learn the rebellion was abortive. Caught by the Linton's dog, she was taken into the Grange and magically transformed into an adult. Heathcliff tries to follow her ('Nelly make me decent, I'm going to be good') but is frustrated, and decides instead to be bad.[5]

Child/adult; bad/good; rebel/conformist. It all seems very simple. If we think of this 'transformation' in terms of the van Ghent approach, we could see it as an attempt by Catherine to become 'human' – that is civilized, socialized, adult. Heathcliff doesn't want her to grow up; he wants her to remain child-like and asocial; he wants to maintain their non-human, 'natural' relationship.

Let's look more closely at the text. While Catherine is at Thrushcross Grange, Mrs Earnshaw visits her often – 'trying to raise her self-respect with fine clothes and flattery' (Ch. 7, p. 93). We have already seen Hindley demonstrating class pretensions by separating 'family' from 'servants', and he has already tried to keep Catherine and Heathcliff apart by emphasizing a difference of class (Ch. 6, pp. 86–7). Now his wife tries to woo Catherine (with *fine clothes* and *flattery*) to become – not a socialized adult, or a civilized human – but a *lady*. 'You look like a lady now', says Hindley (Ch. 7, p. 93).

Catherine is a lady now in dress, manners and social attitudes. Her dress is appropriate to the Grange rather than the Heights: notice how 'she was obliged to hold up with both hands . . . a long cloth habit' which suggests a very cumbersome and clumsy style of dress for a farmhouse. Her fingers are 'wonderfully whitened with doing nothing, and staying in doors' (p. 93) – she has become accustomed to a world where life is centred on the inside of houses, and where, above all, she *does no work*. She's become accustomed to a style of living where class status and privilege place her above those who work for her, produce for her and support her needs; and where her dress, manners, speech and social attitudes separate her absolutely from the inferior class.

The change goes deeper than that. In the first paragraph Nelly expects a 'hatless little savage' who would 'squeeze us all breathless'. Instead of demonstrative affection Catherine now shows passionless reserve. She dare not touch the dogs who come to 'welcome her', because they might dirty her clothes. She can't hug Nelly, she only 'kissed her gently', for the same reason (p. 93). Most important of all, she has changed her attitude to Heathcliff. She embraces him just as affectionately, but she sees matter for concern now in Heathcliff's dirty appearance: 'She gazed concernedly at the dusky fingers she held in her own, and also at her dress, which she feared had gained no embellishment from its contact with his' (Ch. 6, p. 95).

Catherine thinks she can have everything that the other life can offer her – fine clothes, flattery, the status and privilege of a lady – and still retain the older relationship with Heathcliff. But Heathcliff is unable to accept this. 'I shall not stand to be laughed at, I shall not bear it! . . . You needn't have touched me! . . . I shall be as dirty as I please, and I like to be dirty, and I will be dirty' (p. 95). Is Heathcliff's reaction a childish refusal of adult priorities? Or a very natural and healthy reaction based on a rejection of Catherine's new values?

'The eternal rocks beneath'

Please read chapter 9 of *Wuthering Heights*, then consider and make notes on the following questions:
(a) Examine the grounds for Catherine's choice of Edgar rather than Heathcliff. What do you think of her reasons?
(b) Nelly thinks that her 'catechism' of Catherine was 'not injudicious'. Do you agree?
(c) Do you think Nelly understands Catherine's predicament?

DISCUSSION

(a) My own view is that Catherine's reasons are (as Nelly says) very unsuitable ones. She loves Edgar – but then she loves Heathcliff too, in a much more intense and significant way. Edgar is preferred because he is 'handsome, and pleasant to be with', 'young, and cheerful' – but most of all because 'he will be rich, and I shall like to be the greatest woman of the neighbourhood, and I shall be proud of having such a husband' (Ch. 9, p. 118).

(b)   Catherine is now accepting the values of the Thrushcross Grange world. Wealth, position, social distinction – with a bit of love and pleasure thrown in – are the grounds of her attraction to Edgar. Nelly's criticism of Catherine throughout this dialogue (her 'catechism') cuts straight through the superficiality of Catherine's judgements, and ultimately forces her to admit that marriage to Edgar will involve a distortion of her nature: that part of her which is most fundamentally related to Heacliff.

(c)   But is the appropriateness of Nelly's comments based on a complete understanding of Catherine's predicament? To answer this question we should look at the function of Nelly's narrative in this dialogue.

The degree and depth of her understanding seem to fluctuate during this debate. This is a common feature of Emily Brontë's technique: as we have seen, she doesn't use an omniscient narrator, who knows and understands everything, but an actual, credible, knowable person, who lives and moves entirely within the world of the novel. As a character, Nelly is likely to understand some things and fail to understand others. She has no trouble in recognizing how wrong Catherine is to marry Edgar. She is also aware of how the separation will affect Heathcliff. But does she comprehend the nature of Catherine's attachment to Heathcliff? Does she understand what Catherine means by preferring Wuthering Heights to the conventional Christian heaven? Does she not dismiss Catherine's statement of her love as 'nonsense' (Ch. 9, p. 122)? Can we agree with that? Or perhaps Nelly doesn't believe that Catherine can love Heathcliff as she claims, and yet marry Edgar Linton.

We should, I think, be wrong to take everything Nelly says as automatically true. I have shown earlier how Nelly's feelings lead our sympathetic awareness where the author wants it to go. But as she is a fully human character, her understanding may be fallible. For example, though I think Emily Brontë endorses Nelly's sympathy for Heathcliff, she doesn't seem to endorse her religious orthodoxy.

What are we to make of this conflict between the affirmation of love and Nelly's unsympathetic attitude towards it? Possibly Nelly's lack of understanding is an indication to us that the love Catherine speaks of is very difficult to understand. Or possibly

Nelly's comments are intended as a criticism of the intense, passionate and thoughtless love expressed by Catherine: to suggest that if we endorse the love of Catherine and Heathcliff, we have to recognize that it will be disruptive – not only of a false order like that of Thrushcross Grange, but of all existing moral and social values; such love is perhaps by nature anarchic and destructive.

Now please study and make notes on the following passage. How would you define the kind of love Catherine is expressing for Heathcliff? What sort of relationship would such a love imply? Is such a relationship best described as transcendent, or does it involve some of the real human and social concerns we have been exploring earlier in this chapter?

'Every Linton on the face of the earth might melt into nothing, before I could consent to forsake Heathcliff! Oh, that's not what I intend – that's not what I mean! I shouldn't be Mrs Linton were such a price demanded! He'll be as much to me as he has been all his lifetime. Edgar must shake off his antipathy, and tolerate him, at least. He will when he learns my true feelings towards him. Nelly, I see now, you think me a selfish wretch, but did it ever strike you that if Heathcliff and I married, we should be beggars? whereas, if I marry Linton, I can aid Heathcliff to rise, and place him out of my brother's power.'

'With your husband's money, Miss Catherine?' I asked. 'You'll find him not so pliable as you calculate upon: and, though I'm hardly a judge, I think that's the worst motive you've given yet for being the wife of young Linton.'

'It is not', retorted she, 'it is the best! The others were the satisfaction of my whims; and for Edgar's sake, too, to satisfy him. This is for the sake of one who comprehends in his person my feelings to Edgar and myself. I cannot express it; but surely you and everybody have a notion that there is, or should be, an existence of yours beyond you. What were the use of my creation if I were entirely contained here? My great miseries in this world have been Heathcliff's miseries, and I watched and felt each from the beginning; my great thought in living is himself. If all else perished, and *he* remained, I should still continue to be; and, if all else remained, and he were annihilated, the universe would turn to a mighty stranger. I should not seem a part of it. My love for Linton is like the foliage in the woods. Time will change it, I'm well aware, as winter changes the trees – my love for Heathcliff resembles the eternal rocks beneath – a source of little visible delight, but necessary. Nelly, I *am* Heathcliff – he's always, always in my mind – not as a pleasure, any more than I am always a pleasure to myself – but, as my own being . . . (Ch. 9, pp. 121–2)

DISCUSSION

Below I have provided five different arguments about the nature of the love between Catherine and Heathcliff, followed by my own discussion. I have defined the different approaches as (a) the 'romantic'; (b) the 'historical'; (c) the 'religious'; (d) the 'psychoanalytic'; (e) the 'feminist'. Compare and consider these different views, and try to use them to work out some ideas and opinions of your own.

(a)   It is common for critics to talk about the relationship between *Wuthering Heights* and the Romantic movement of the late eighteenth and early nineteenth centuries. They point to Emily Brontë's use of certain familiar Romantic images, such as the child or the 'Byronic hero'; the use of landscape, the connection of nature with emotional moods and moral values, the use of dreams, of the supernatural, and of effects which could be described as 'Gothic'.[6]

Another familiar notion of the book's 'romantic' quality is the popular concept of 'romance' as a love story with an emphasis on passion and intense feeling. In the light of this approach, we could say that the love of Catherine and Heathcliff is romantic because it is intense, passionate and absolute. It is everything that love generally is *not* in ordinary life. In life we love, and cherish, often till death us do part; but we don't embrace to music on misty mountain tops, or sing Liebestods, or drink poison out of the same cup. In life passion exists, not in an abstract and refined form, but inextricably involved with all the other aspects of relationship, and with the day-to-day material realities of ordinary life. The pure devotion of Catherine and Heathcliff fascinates us because it's something we can't often achieve, and can certainly never sustain. We could say that it is a form of escapism.[7]

(b)   A more *historical* approach would remind us that the Romantic movement was not merely a literary movement, but also a *social* one; and that an emphasis on intense feeling is something that emerged in response to a process of social change, and from writers who felt that society was working to dehumanize or destroy or pervert 'natural' relationship and 'natural' feeling. A novelist writing in such a society would naturally place a high premium on feeling and relationship. As Raymond Williams says:

> The world we need to remember if we are to see these conditions of the 1840's is the world of Blake: a world of desire and hunger, of rebellion and of pallid convention: the terms of desire and the terms of oppression connected in a single dimension of experience.
>
> Nobody later achieved Blake's kind of unity; he could only barely maintain it himself. But I think we need to start from the

feeling, the central feeling, that an intensity of desire is as much a response, a deciding response, to the human crisis of that time as the more obviously recognizable political radicalism. Indeed, to give that kind of value to human longing and need, to that absolute emphasis on commitment to another, the absolute love of the being of another, is to clash as sharply with the emerging system, the emerging priorities, as in any assault on material poverty. What was at issue really was relationship itself: a dimension of relationship made problematic and dangerous by the increasing pressure, the external and internal and continuing pressure, to reshape, to deform – it is how Blake saw it – this most human, most absolute experience.[8]

Raymond Williams sees nothing 'romantic' in the escapist sense in Catherine's love. It is a familar aspect of ordinary human experience.

These words of Cathy have been called mystical, or a romantic extravagance. But I don't know how that can be said if we listen and follow the action. That kind of bond, that sense of absolute presence, absolute existence in another, in one another, is indeed an ordinary though of course always a transforming experience. In many lives, again and again, it is the central reality of everything else that happens, and indeed quite often doesn't need to be emphasized: the reality of the relationship is simply there and unbreakable. (p. 66)

(c) Other critics have argued that the most important thing about the love of Catherine and Heathcliff is that it is not *romantic* or *historical*, but religious. 'Surely you and everybody have a notion that there is, or should be, an existence of your beyond you' says Catherine (Ch. 9, p. 122). Their relationship is one of the soul, a spiritual relationship. It is therefore as *external* as the rocks beneath because it transcends time and material existence. All flesh is grass; flowers and foliage and Edgar Linton fade, but the love of Catherine and Heathcliff endureth for ever.

Like so many pairs of romantic lovers Catherine and Heathcliff are, so to speak, consecrated one to another, each feeling his or her passion as the consuming reality of existence. What is undeniably personal, however, in the manner of their love is the peculiar, almost religious intensity with which it is expressed and which perhaps finds its most significant manifestation in Catherine's attempt to explain her feelings to Nelly Dean.
     The nature of Emily Brontë's experience of life, here perhaps expresed more directly than elsewhere, was religious in type: religious not merely in the sense of the rather indefinite 'mysticism' which has often been conceded to her on the strength of isolated passages in her poems, but in an awareness, at once more clear-cut and more open to definition, of the necessary incompleteness of all the elements that go to make up human nature in its time-conditioned state.[9]

(d)   I return again to the Freudian approach of Dorothy van Ghent. Her argument would suggest that arguments (a), (b) and (c) all suffer from the same misconception – that the love of Catherine and Heathcliff is a kind of human love. It is in fact, for her *non-human*. *Wuthering Heights* is a book irrelevant to the social and moral reason: the attitude to life implicit in it is rather one of 'awed contemplation of an unregenerate universe than a feeling for values and disvalues in types of human intercourse' (p. 153).

Heathcliff is, to van Ghent, an elemental figure, presented naked of civilized habits and ways of feeling, occupying an equivocal status on the edge of the human. The passions in *Wuthering Heights* are too simple, too undeviating in intensity to find an echo in practical social reality. Catherine and Heathcliff are not adult 'characters': the complex attendant motivations of adult life, the recognition of the domestic and social responsibilities, the spiritual complexities of adult life are all lacking. They are in fact portions of the flux of nature, trying to identify themselves as human, but disrupting life by their appetite for an inhuman kind of intercourse. A possible form of relationship for them would have to be asocial, amoral, savagely irresponsible. They become caught in the economic forms of social life – Catherine in marriage and Heathcliff in property relations – but their passion is always inhuman, the desire to lose the self in otherness. In Catherine and Heathcliff the regressive desire is pure, and opens up the prospect of disintegration into childhood unconsciousness or death – that is, into anonymous natural energy.

(e)   Finally I would like to introduce you to a feminist reading of *Wuthering Heights*. Feminist criticism, which is discussed at greater length in Chapter 7 of this *Guide*, is one of the most original and interesting developments in modern literary studies. Patricia Meyer Spacks, author of *The Female Imagination*, concentrates her attention on Catherine rather than Heathcliff. She sees Catherine as a subversive creation, 'in every respect opposed to her century's ideal prototype of the adolescent woman . . . she embodies the adolescent as revolutionary, articulating a new set of values for the heroine, interesting precisely for her nonconformity'. Heathcliff becomes almost incidental to the argument of this critic, who sees Catherine as a figure peculiarly eloquent of the oppressed position of Victorian women:

> Heathcliff is partly a figment of Catherine's imagination as well as of Emily Brontë's. Catherine's fantasies, . . . are focused on Heathcliff: if he were not there, she would have to invent him. In fact she does invent him, directly and indirectly shaping his being.

... The position of the adolescent woman epitomises that of women in general, limited in opportunity by the assumptions of society, forced toward indirection to retain an illusion of force. The theme of adolescence has special poignance for women, the fate of that defiance being, almost always, to fail at last.[10]

You may find these differing views very illuminating. You may find them confusing, and that would be understandable. The thing to do now is to sort out what *you* think about this matter. Does that love seem to you 'escapist', or 'religious', or 'a normal part of everyday experience', or 'a non-human form of intercourse'? Don't think of these different attitudes as mutually exclusive – or as in any way exhausting the possibilities of response. The answer might be a combination of different views, or different from any of them. And the main thing to remember is that the 'answer' is not an absolute and definitive 'solution' to the problem – the answer will be your answer, formed by your own experience of reading the novel.

Let us now look at the five different views of Catherine and Heathcliff's love. Is it not the case that the simple 'romantic' view of their love, though perhaps a reasonable *description*, is not an adequate *understanding* of its nature? Whatever the nature of the love itself, it is explored within a 'realistic' context: the novel shows that love is inextricably involved with all the other aspects of relationship, and with the day-to-day material realities of ordinary life.

For the same reasons I would reject Dorothy van Ghent's interpretation, which talks of Catherine and Heathcliff being 'caught' in social life like wild animals in a cage. The novel's technique of composing a synthesis of conventions ensures that 'realism' is taken as seriously as 'romance', and that we recognize the characters' social existence to be as real as their spiritual life. (For further discussion of this see Chapter 6 of the *Guide*.)

The *religious* interpretation is also, I think, unsatisfactory: Catherine talks of 'an existence of yours beyond you', but her 'extended soul' (Ch. 9, p. 122) is simply another human being, Heathcliff; and her dream of going to heaven contains an explicit *rejection* of religious values – 'heaven did not seem to be my home . . . '(Ch. 9, p. 120). In fact the use of the word 'religion' in the passage quoted from Derek Traversi is a very vague and loose usage, in which the word is abstracted not only from the context of religious institutions and practices, but from the context of any specific body or religious beliefs. Whether used in an orthodox or unorthdox way, the word 'religious' does not, I feel, help us very much.

Of the five proferred arguments, I prefer (b), which relates the novel's 'emphasis on intense feeling' to the Romantic movement and to the historical developments of the late eighteenth and nineteenth centuries; and (e), which also seeks to elucidate the novel's conflicts and problems in the light of a historical attention to the real conflicts and problems of Victorian society; though you may feel, as I do, that the attempted exclusion of Heathcliff from the argument is perhaps a distortion of the novel. Would Catherine herself have rebelled so forcefully against the values of her society without the assistance of the social outsider Heathcliff?

The love of Catherine and Heathcliff cannot, of course, be *reduced* to general social and historical facts, but the novel itself insists on *placing* it *within* such a context:

> . . . the choice posed for Catherine between Heathcliff and Edgar Linton . . . seems to me the pivotal event of the novel, the decisive catalyst of the tragedy; and if this is so, then the crux of *Wuthering Heights* must be conceded by even the most remorselessly mytho-logical and mystical of critics to be a social one. In a crucial act of self-betrayal and bad faith, Catherine rejects Heathcliff as a suitor because he is socially inferior to Linton; and it is from this that the train of destruction follows.[11]

The emphasis on intense individual passion is a characteristic note of the 'romanticism' of the Brontë novels generally. The heroine of *Jane Eyre* demands love, of an intense and passionate kind, as a means of bringing satisfaction to a life frustrated by the powerful pressure of social forces. And in *Wuthering Heights* too, the demand for absolute love is a direct challenge to those social forces of family and class which tyrannize, oppress and restrict individuals and their relationships. The primacy of individual passion goes back, as Raymond Williams says, to Romanticism; and particularly to the individualism of the Romantic revolt, which in turn expressed the *contradictory* quality of the bourgeois-democratic revolutions of the later eighteenth and early nineteenth centuries. The ascendant bourgeois class sought general social liberation, but in practice remained trapped with an ideology of individualism, which led to the betrayal of its expressed aspiration towards universal freedom. In these novels of the later 1840s the powerful individualism of Romanticism is now much more problematical, fraught with conflict and contradiction, even in *Wuthering Heights* pushing towards a tragic resolution – as if it seemed no longer possible to identify individual with social aspiration and fulfilment. The bourgeoisie was now embattled: on the one side threatened by a militant working class, on the other subjected to radical criticism by an ideologically powerful though politically weakened aristocracy. The demand for individual fulfilment and the possibilities for social harmony and regeneration appear in literature as complex patterns of resolution and conflict, especially in Charlotte Brontë's novel of love and industrial struggle, *Shirley* (1849). The demand for love and individual fulfilment is no timeless 'romantic' abstraction, but a response to concrete historical conditions. *Wuthering Heights* always insists that 'romantic' love should never be seen as detachable from the real social conditions which it rejects and denies, yet with which it is inseparably connected.

Even if we grant that the love of Catherine and Heathcliff is always *placed* within a social context, it is still possible to argue that 'romantic' love is nonetheless affirmed and endorsed by the novel as an absolute and unquestionable value. Is Catherine simply swayed against her real nature by social pressures; or is there something about the quality of her love that leads her to make the wrong decision? Is that love seen in the novel as absolute and irreducible, or is it seen as internally contradictory and therefore vulnerable in itself?

Catherine's account of her love emphasizes the intimacy of the relationship, which is so close as to almost *identify* her with Heathcliff. 'Nelly, I *am* Heathcliff' (Ch. 9, p. 122) seems to express the most absolute degree of devotion and commitment. That is the most 'romantic' aspect of the love; it is also the most dangerous. If Heathcliff is not a separate individual but a part of Catherine's nature, then there cannot possibly be any separation between them; Catherine can even marry Edgar without violating the bond. Catherine's conception of love denies Heathcliff his independent individuality, his 'otherness', and that denial must, clearly, be fatally destructive to any relationship. In fact Catherine refuses to respect Linton's individuality as well, in believing that he will accept Heathcliff as a partner in her affections. She believes that Linton is subordinate to her, and that Heathcliff is part of her; whatever decision she may make, she feels, will carry them along with it. She is of course very wrong: both Heathcliff (immediately) and Linton (eventually) find it necessary to assert their individual integrity against her.

> 'I *am* Heathcliff!' is dramatically arresting, but it is also a way of keeping the outcast at arm's length, evading the challenge he offers. If Catherine is Heathcliff – if identity rather than relationship is in question – then their estrangement is inconceivable, and Catherine can therefore turn to others without violating the timeless metaphysical idea Heathcliff embodies ... Heathcliff, understandably, refuses to settle for this ... [12]

Romantic love, then, is not only set within a context of social and domestic reality in which its values are questioned and qualified; the very essence of romantic love is here subjected to a keen cross-questioning which discloses within it a fatally destructive contradiction – that, by its emphasis on merging and identification, it denies the independent validity of the lovers' existence.

I have expressed my own view here as clearly and as polemically as possible, so that there will be less danger of you accepting it uncritically as the 'correct answer', the solution, the appropriate synthesis of all other views. You should think of it in the same way as you think of the other arguments that are merely quoted here. It may well be that one of them seems to you more consistent with your personal response to the novel, in which case you would wish to read and appreciate it more fully by pursuing my references to their original source. Ultimately you should be *using* these arguments as the raw material for the composition of your own authentic, individual and personal vision of *Wuthering Heights*.

4. The Language

Discussing the 'language' of fiction has recently come to cover a considerable variety of activities. Attempts have been made to draw literary criticism into the science of linguistics, basing the study of literature on more analytical and philosophical principles than the more familiar methods of 'reading', 'appreciation', 'criticism' of particular texts. Modern linguistic criticism can be more interested in a literary text as a function of language, as a cultural product which has its place in the practices of communication which help to compose and maintain a particular form of society; interested in the general functioning of language in society, rather than in the special unique qualities of a specific literary work.[1]

These developments are interesting and important: but particular texts remain the basic material of literary study, and valuable work can be done with the more traditional approach to language, which consists simply in a very close attention to the novelist's particular way of handling words, and to the function of language in constructing the novel's totality of meanings. As the language is the medium through which everything in the novel is communicated to us, the physical signs that actually touch our senses and activate our imaginations, analysis is initially a matter of becoming more aware of what is before us all the time as we read.

We have already examined one example of the novel's use of language: Lockwood's account of his experience by the sea-coast. Pursuing there the specific qualities of Lockwood's language, the stilted 'literariness' of his speech, we found that the language is both a characterization of the man, and a means of establishing the cultural differences between himself and the social world he is entering. Though only one of the four residents of the Heights (Joseph) speaks in regional dialect, and Heathcliff is able to address Lockwood with elaborate politeness, the stranger is constantly confronted with a stark directness of speech which contrasts sharply with his own circumlocutory discourse, and frequently dislocates his sense of propriety, of 'normality' as he knows it. Notice the differences of language in the following exchanges of dialogue:

(a) *Heathcliff:* 'What the devil is the matter?'
    Lockwood: 'The herd of possessed swine could have had no worse spirits in them than those animals of yours, sir.' (Ch. 1, p. 49)
(b) *Lockwood:* 'I'm afraid, Mrs Heathcliff, the floor must bear the consequences of your servants' leisure attendance.'
    Hareton: 'Sit down! . . . He'll be in soon.' (Ch. 1, p. 52)
(c) *Lockwood:* 'A beautiful animal! Do you intend parting with the little ones, madam?'
    Cathy: 'They are not mine!' (Ch. 1, p. 52)
(d) *Lockwood:* 'Ah, certainly – I see now; you are the favoured possessor of the benificient fairy?'
    Hareton: 'My name is Hareton Earnshaw, and I'd counsel you to respect it!' (Ch. 1, pp. 55–6).

This sustained contrast between the two cultures, the native and the stranger's, is not limited to dialogue. Study and make notes on the following passage, defining the differences between the language of the two paragraphs.

On that black hill-top the earth was hard with a black frost, and the air made me shiver through every limb. Being unable to remove the chain, I jumped over, and, running up the flagged causeway bordered with straggling gooseberry bushes, knocked vainly for admittance, till my knuckles tingled, and the dogs howled.

'Wretched inmates!' I ejaculated, mentally, 'you deserve perpetual isolation from your species for your churlish inhospitality. At least, I would not keep my doors barred in the day time – I don't care – I will get in!' (Ch. 2, p. 51).

DISCUSSION

Lockwood's speech is again pompous, mannered, 'bookish'. By contrast the language of the first paragraph *seems* very close to 'reality'. The combination in the first paragraph of simple, vivid words such as 'bleak', 'black'; verbs of action and movement such as 'shiver', 'jumped', 'running', 'knocked'; and precise descriptive details such as the 'flagged causeway bordered with straggling gooseberry bushes', 'my knuckles tingled', 'the dogs howled': all these activate the reader's sensory perceptions to create the illusion of the 'real' experience enacted, or even 'lived through': as if the writing had the power to transport the reader, immersed in a book, to some real place and time.

In actual fact, of course, that language of 'real experience' is no less 'literary' than Lockwood's: the apparently 'concrete', sensory evocation of experience is also a literary device, impossible to confuse *with* physical experience (we don't in fact acquire breathlessness or tingling in the knuckles from *reading* an account of physical exertion). Nevertheless I think we could say that the kinds of language used in these two paragraphs are distinct: while Lockwood's speech works on an inflated rhetorical level ('wretched inmates', 'perpetual isolation'), the descriptive prose conveys an illusion of physical sensation, by using words that (mainly because of their use in common speech) *seem* close to actuality. The contrast is also, we should observe, a kind of trick: since Lockwood, as narrator, is literally the 'author' of both passages. One kind of language though seems to take our attention outwards towards the external world (it is 'representational'); the other forces our attention back towards the man who produces it.

We've seen that Lockwood reveals his character by using stilted, literary language. He almost expects people to behave as they do in books: remember how he 'warmed towards' Heathcliff when he thought he was acting the part of a misanthropist, but was shocked when Heathcliff revealed a '*genuine* bad nature'. This is how one critic puts it:

There is something basically wrong, which is reflected in Lockwood's diction. He expects (and wants) people to behave as they do in novels; he wants life to imitate a certain kind of art in the way in which life often does when people follow conventional roles in order to structure their experience. But these are people who do not choose to behave that way, and Lockwood is as helpless and lost as the reader expecting a conventional literary experience.[2]

The distinction proposed here between 'convention' and 'experience' produces difficulties similar to those involved in the contrasting of 'literary' and 'experiential' language. A lot of traditional literary criticism (deriving ultimately from positivist philosophies of the nineteenth century) supposes that certain kinds of literary language can give a reader direct access to experience: if the language of a text is successful, it can represent the real world in a truthful, accurate and illuminating way. Literary language that *fails* produces a false, distorted, artificial view of the world. Post-structuralist literary theory maintains that language is always constructing its own versions of reality, which are *ideological*: that is, they *appear* to be imitations or representations of a reality that has an objective existence outside them; but in fact they are constructions, visions of the world invented by particular individuals, classes or societies.[3] In the light of these theoretical ideas, the difference between artifice and truth, or illusion and reality, is only a difference between two distinct and in some ways antagonistic ideological visions of the world. Similarly, a sociologist might question the distinction proposed in the passage quoted above: isn't *all* our experience structured by conventional roles, even when we behave 'unconventionally'? Nevertheless, the notion of 'convention' seems to me a useful one. The *conventions* of life at Wuthering Heights constitute a distinct and recognizable way of life, influenced by certain general and particular determinants: such as a relation to agricultural labour, geographical isolation, Heathcliff's establishment of an unusual 'family' structure. These conventions, and the language in which they are expressed, seem utterly foreign and unintelligible to Lockwood, whose experience is structured by the conventions of civilized intercourse and the discourses of politeness. Both cultures are equally 'real': but each has an entirely different view of the world, an entirely different grasp on experience.

Look now at the passage below. Again, what differences do you notice between the first paragraph and the rest?

"'T' maister nobbut just buried, and Sabbath nut o'ered, und t' sahnd uh t' gospel still i' yer lugs, and yah darr be laiking! shame on

ye! sit ye dahn, ill childer! they's good books eneugh if ye'll read
'em; sit ye dahn, and think uh yer sowls!"'

'Saying this, he compelled us so to square our positions that we
might receive, from the far-off fire, a dull ray to show us the text of
the lumber he thrust upon us.

'I could not bear the employment. I took my dingy volume by
the scroop, and hurled it into the dog-kennel, vowing I hated a good
book.

'Heathcliff kicked his to the same place.

'Then there was a hubbub! (Ch. 3, p. 63)

DISCUSSION

Obviously Joseph's dialect is different from the language Catherine
uses. But aren't there points of contact between the dialect and
Catherine's speech? Again we find strongly physical, active verbs:
'square', 'hurled', 'kicked'; and expressive adjectives such as
'dull' and 'dingy'. But the main thing I think is that the movement,
tone, texture of Catherine's speech have a physical quality and a
sensory vigour comparable to the concreteness of the dialect – 'the
lumber he *thrust* upon us'; 'I took my dingy volume by the scroop';
'hurled it into the dog-kennel'; 'Heathcliff kicked his to the same
place'; 'then there was a hubbub!'.

The narrator in that particular passage was of course
Catherine, writing the 'diary' that Lockwood subsequently reads.
The language she uses as a child suggests that her relationship with
the material reality of her environment is closer, stronger, more
immediate than (for example) the relationship indicated by
Lockwood's speech. We can find a similar sense of affinity between
narration and reality in the reported speech of Heathcliff. Study
and make notes on the following passage from Heathcliff's account
of the visit to Thrushcross Grange. Does it seem to you that the
language is a convincing and realistic representation of the young
Heathcliff's possible style of narration?

> '"Run, Heathcliff, run!" she whispered. "They have let the bull-dog
> loose, and he holds me!"
> 'The devil had siezed her ankle, Nelly; I heard his abominable
> snorting. She did not yell out – no! She would have scorned to do it,
> if she had been spitted on the horns of a mad cow. I did, though, I
> vociferated curses enough to annihilate any fiend in Christendom,
> and I got a stone and thrust it between his jaws, and tried with all
> my might to cram it down his throat ..   (Ch. 6, p. 90)

DISCUSSION

Put like that, the answer must be 'no': this is not naturalistic dialogue. 'I vociferated curses enough to annihilate any fiend in Christendom' is as distant from colloquial or dialect speech as any of Lockwood's flights of rhetoric. But as in the previous passage, the dialogue contains a calculated emphasis on violent and harsh vocabulary, with many verbs of energetic action and movement – *Run, hold, siezed, snorting, yell, spitted, thrust, cram*: and a high intensity of physical violence enacted in the language:

> 'I got a stone and *thrust it between his jaws,* and tried with all my might to *cram it down his throat'.* (p. 90)

If such words were attributed, say, to a gentlemanly character from a Jane Austen novel, fashionably lounging in the Assembly rooms at Bath, we would feel that something was wrong: the character would be affecting a melodramatic violence of language out of key with the manners of his environment. In Heathcliff's mouth they seem appropriate, and moreover singularly in keeping with his immediate context. The children have just witnessed a scene of violence (the quarrel between the Linton children) and responded by parodying it with their satirical mockery. Thrushcross Grange reacts to that challenge with an astonishing display of violence – dogs, guns, and even prisons and the gallows are employed or alluded to. The violence of the Lintons' power is however concealed by the veneer of civilization – their language keeps violence firmly *outside*:

> *Isabella*: '"Frightful thing! Put him in the cellar, papa. He's exactly like the son of the fortune-teller, that stole my tame pheasant."
> *Mrs Linton*: '"A wicked boy, at all events . . . and quite unfit for a decent house! Did you notice his language, Linton? I'm shocked that my children should have heard it." (Ch. 6, p. 91)

By this stage Heathcliff's 'language' has been reduced to inarticulate swearing – 'I recommenced cursing' – but the harsh and violent directness of his speech seems to express the truth of the situtation, while the language of the Lintons mystifies *their* violence by attributing it to the outsider.

An account of the languages used by different narrators is not complete without some references to Nelly Dean. Lockwood characterizes her speech as a species of standard english: 'Excepting a few provincialisms of slight consequence, you have no marks of the manners that I am habituated to consider as peculiar to your class' (Ch. 7, p. 103). And we have already observed at least two critics identifying Nelly and Lockwood as indistinguishable witnesses. Another critic argues that they even share a common language:

Rather than being opposite to one another, Nelly and Lockwood are very much alike and speak in remarkably similar fashion. To translate Lockwood into a type called City Man and Nelly into another marked Country Servant, and to see them, then, as representatives of opposing principles and life-styles is to ignore the evidence of their speech. Any observation we may make about Lockwood's diction is almost certainly equally true of Nelly's. The differences in their backgrounds and education seem, therefore, quite irrelevant, for those differences have led only to sameness. In Nelly and Lockwood, country and town share a single bland speech.[4]

Study and make notes on the following passage in the light of this statement. Does it seem to you to confirm the critic's view?

> We crowded round, and over Miss Cathy's head I had a peep at a dirty, ragged, black-haired child; big enough both to walk and talk – indeed, its face looked older than Catherine's – yet, when it was set on its feet, it only stared round, and repeated over and over again some gibberish that nobody could understand. I was frightened, and Mrs Earnshaw was ready to fling it out of doors: she did fly up – asking how could he fashion to bring that gipsy brat into the house, when they had their own bairns to feed, and fend for? What he meant to do with it, and whether he were mad? (Ch. 4, pp. 77–8)

There is hardly any formal distinction there between the prose and the reported speech: Nelly's narrative prose, dramatic and colloquial – 'some gibberish that nobody could understand'; 'to fling it out of doors'; 'she *did* fly up' – is almost indistinguishable in structure, rhythm and diction from Mrs Earnshaw's dialect. Nelly seems to *belong* to the world of the Heights as much as Lockwood belongs to a completely separate world of metropolitan civilization and culture; a culture to which Thrushcross Grange is affiliated. The language emphasizes rather than minimizes the difference between town and country, gentleman and servant, city and provincial life. Suppose Nelly had narrated the opening of the novel instead of Lockwood: would we have had the same impression of Wuthering Heights and of Heathcliff? Obviously not: how then can Lockwood and Nelly both represent a common, central, recognizable 'normality'?

Both language and narrative technique seem to be employed here to the same purpose: to establish a structural pattern – the figure of an ignorant stranger entering an unfamiliar society – which is as fundamental to Emily Brontë's novel as it is to the fiction of Sir Walter Scott or Thomas Hardy. The collisions produced by such 'invasions' express and dramatize the cultural

conflicts within a society: both narrative and language operate in
Wuthering Heights to distinguish and oppose city and country,
south and north, gentleman and servant, urban and rural gentry,
fashionable and traditional manners; above all, perhaps, the
contrast opens out the gulf between the inhibited shyness of
Lockwood's personal relations, and the deep passions of love,
hatred and revenge that are scarcely concealed in the inhabitants of
Wuthering Heights.

I would like you, before we leave this topic, to consider a
different view of Nelly Dean's language. Please read the closing
pages of Chapter 7 of *Wuthering Heights* (pp. 102–3). Then study
and make notes on the following passage. What do you make of
Lockwood's observations on Nelly's command of language? How
does this compare with what I've been saying about her discourse?

> 'Excepting a few provincialisms of slight consequence, you have no
> marks of the manners which I am habituated to consider as peculiar
> to your class. I am sure you have thought a great deal more than the
> generality of servants think. You have been compelled to cultivate
> your reflective faculties, for want of occasion for frittering your life
> away in silly trifles.' (Ch. 7, p. 103)

Consider also this passage from a critic who offers an entirely
different view of Nelly's linguistic character from the one I have
been proposing:[5]

> The real mediation in the work, however, is Nelly Deans's
> narration: it is this that Lockwood interposes between himself and
> the labyrinth of the Heights. It is the role she performs as insulating
> mediator that makes Nelly the real villain of the piece for she is the
> literacy that prevents the reading of the self and the experience of the
> other . . . for Nelly is that standard language required by the
> bourgeoisie to mediate and dissolve its contradictions.

The critic then quotes Lockwood's description, cited above, of
Nelly's discourse, and comments

> What a paradigmatic model of liberal education! The limits are set so
> precisely: from the remaining trace of provincialism to the ability at
> least . . . to distinguish foreign books by their covers.

The critic's language is perhaps difficult and unfamiliar: I will be
saying more about his interesting argument in my Chapter 7. The
main point is that he sees Nelly Dean's language as an *educated*
provincialism, standard English with a slight regional flavour.
Lockwood admires her discourse because it is compatible with his
own – they share a common language. Nelly is seen as a mediator
between Wuthering Heights and Lockwood, just as the imposition

of a standard English by universal education mediated (in this critic's Marxist view) between the antagonistic classes of Victorian society.

Now read this passage from Chapter 32: Nelly's opinion of the marriage of Catherine and Hareton. Examine Nelly's language carefully. Is it the language of a Yorkshire servant, intimately bound up with the life of the region? or the standard English of a 'liberal education'?

> The intimacy thus commenced, grew rapidly; though it encountered temporary interruptions. Earnshaw was not to be civilized with a wish; and my young lady was no philosopher, and no paragon of patience; but both their minds tending to the same point – one loving and desiring to esteem; and the other loving and desiring to be esteemed – they contrived in the end, to reach it.
>
> You see, Mr Lockwood, it was easy enough to win Mrs Heathcliff's heart; but now, I'm glad you did not try – the crown of all my wishes will be the union of those two; I shall envy no one on their wedding day – there won't be a happier woman than myself in England! (Ch. 32, p. 346)

DISCUSSION

It is surely an urbane and civilized discourse, the language of education, of 'civilization', of the 'centre'. The structure of Nelly's sentences is quite complex, with at least one latinate construction ('The intimacy thus commenced'). She handles concepts such as that of the 'philosopher' with apparent ease and familiarity; and speaks confidently from a position of 'civilization' about one (Hareton) who has yet to attain it. The emphasis of both form and meaning is all on mediation – uniting, harmonizing, resolution. The pattern of words in the second paragraph – crown, union, wedding day, England – have an intensely centralizing effect: showing that Nelly sees herself as a citizen of England, not a native of Yorkshire; as a member of Lockwood's 'national' culture, not a cultural outsider like Heathcliff.

You can see then that the figure of Nelly is not as simple as she makes herself out to be. There is a deep contradiction in her position, divided between two cultures, a contradiction which her narrative and her language exist to resolve. I will be coming back to this aspect of Nelly; perhaps you would like to ponder it further by reading the closing pages of the novel, and noting her attitude towards the local superstitions (Ch. 34, pp. 366–7). This passage is discussed in full in my next Chapter.

5. Novel or Romance?

In novels that we think of as typical, like those of Jane Austen, plot and dialogue are closely linked to the conventions of the comedy of manners. The conventions of *Wuthering Heights* are linked rather with the tale and the ballad. They seem to have more affinity with tragedy, and the tragic emotions of passion and fury, which would shatter the balance of tone in Jane Austen, can be safely accommodated here. So can the supernatural, or the suggestion of it, which is difficult to get into a novel. The shape of the plot is different: instead of manouvering around a central situation, as Jane Austen does, Emily Brontë tells her story with linear accents, and she seems to need the help of a narrator, who would be absurdly out of place in Jane Austen. Conventions so different justify us in regarding *Wuthering Heights* as a different form of prose fiction from the novel, a form which we shall here call the romance. Here again we have to use the same word in several different contexts, but romance seems on the whole better than tale, which appears to fit a somewhat shorter form.

The essential difference between novel and romance lies in the conception of characterization. The romancer does not attempt to create 'real people' so much as stylized figures which expand into psychological archetypes. It is in the romance that we find Jung's libido, anima, and shadow reflected in the hero, heroine, and villain respectively. That is why the romance so often radiates a glow of subjective intensity that the novel lacks, and why a suggestion of allegory is constantly creeping in around its fringes. Certain elements of character are released in the romance which makes it naturally a more revolutionary form than the novel. The novelist deals with personality, with characters wearing their personae or social masks. He needs the framework of a stable society, and many of our best novelists have been conventional to the verge of fussiness. The romancer deals with individuality, with character *in vacuo* idealized by revery, and, however conservative he may be, something nihilistic and untamable is likely to keep breaking out of his pages.[1]

I have already proposed, in the chapter on Heathcliff, a distinction similar to the one made here by Northrop Frye: my contrast between *realistic* and *fantastic* writing corresponds to Frye's separation of novel and romance. I have taken it for granted by referring to *Wuthering Heights* as a novel, that this is the kind of fiction it is. But clearly *Wuthering Heights* differs so strikingly from many typical nineteenth-century novels that Northrop Frye would wish to classify it as a separate form; and many readers will perhaps concur, in expectation if not in experience, with the view that *Wuthering Heights* is a 'romance'.

Does it matter? – So we tend to ask of such theoretical questions; surely the book is, explicitly and irreducibly, what it is, and whether we call it novel, romance, tale or whatever won't make the slightest difference to the way we read it. We can all (we may say with some exasperation and hurt pride) read, can't we?

Reading any novel, experiencing any work of art, is never quite such a natural activity; but then neither, if you think about it, is communicating by speech or writing a letter. All these activities involve not only the knowledge of a language, but the learning and acceptance of certain *conventions*. In social life a convention is an accepted code of manners and behaviour; in a work of literature it is a particular code of techniques and styles, usually implying a particular set of attitudes towards experience, within which the artist chooses to operate. In novels that are thought of as classically 'realist' in manner, such as those of Tolstoy, the novel is attempting to give the reader the impression that it is 'imitating life' in a very direct way – that the events we are reading about are very close to the common flow of everyday experience. 'Realism', as the word is most often used in modern literary criticism, is just as much a convention as any other; but it's a convention which encourages the reader to imagine that the distance between the novel and 'real life' is a very small or even non-existent. The main point about the use of realism as a convention is that the reader is drawn into a fictional world which seems to be just like the real world. The author does as little as possible to make his audience conscious that what he is reading is a fictional artefact as opposed to life itself. The novel, with its continuous narrative form (a technique which coincides with our way of experiencing and thinking about life in time), and its prose style (which can approximate, especially when used in conjunction with a 'conversational' narrative voice, to ordinary speech) can convey this illusion very successfully. Other kinds of literature declare their distance from real life much more explicitly: poetry, for example, or Shakespeare's drama. Tom Stoppard's

'Player' in *Rosencrantz and Guildenstern are Dead* draws attention
to the conventionality of plays such as *Hamlet*.

> There we were – demented children mincing about in clothes that no
> one ever wore, speaking as no man ever spoke, swearing love in wigs
> and rhymed couplets, killing each other with wooden swords,
> hollow protestations of faith hurled after empty promises of
> vengeance – and every gesture, every pose, vanishing into the thin,
> unpopulated air.[2]

And of course the conventions do seem absurd, when abstracted
from their context and set into an incongruous juxtaposition. When
watching and listening to *Hamlet*, we have to accept them, to an
extent, without question. But to do even this, we have to know the
conventions or at least be prepared for them; and if we wish to
understand a novel as fully as possible, we need a self-conscious
awareness and understanding of the conventions in which it is
written.

Northrop Frye mentions a number of techniques and formal
characteristics that can be used to define the conventions of
Wuthering Heights – plot, dialogue and narrative method; tragedy,
tragic emotion and the supernatural. He connects Jane Austen's
conventions with the comedy of manners; Emily Brontë's with the
more primitive, popular forms of tale and ballad. That contrast can
easily be illustrated by considering differences in narrative method.
In a novel with an impersonal narrator a voice, constantly present,
continually assures and reassures the reader that the entire
experience of the novel, the characters and their social world, are
possessed by a single consciousness with a full understanding and
firm judgement of everything the reader is brought to 'know'. Now
in *Wuthering Heights*, there is no such reliable and omniscient
narrator – and the author, whose 'persona' the narrator is, remains
completely hidden. Such a technique introduces the reader to a
world that is less secure, certain, solid, 'knowable'; a world where
characters and forces seem to operate independently of moral
convention and judgement; a world where 'reality' is much more
fluid and changeable; and where what we '*know*' (or think we
know) is constantly being exploded by the interruption and
invasion of something unknown. Clearly *this* important difference
of technique opens up, to some extent, Frye's distinction between
'novel' and 'romance': the novel insists on the solid reality of its
social and human world, while the romance admits that we cannot
really ever be quite so sure of what we 'know', what is 'real', what
is 'true'.

Frye's distinction between 'novel' and 'romance', useful as it is
for discriminating between different kinds of novel, and between
different conventions at work in the same novel, is nevertheless a
very problematical one. The problems partly stem from the
complexities of such words as 'romance', 'romantic' and
'Romanticism'; but also from Frye's own theoretical strategy,
which is extremely *formalistic* – that is, it attempts to study,
analyse and classify literary productions solely in terms of their
formal properties, outside any historical context; as if novels, plays
and poems belonged to some timeless abstraction known as
'literature', which develops autonomously according to its own
internal laws. We can see how generalizing and abstract Frye's
terminology is by defining the term 'romance' more exactly: it
refers to a specific literary form, the prose and verse tales of
chivalry and love which appeared at a particular period in
mediaeval European history. Clearly *Wuthering Heights* has little
in common with those. I have already suggested that it owes much
to the *Romanticism* of the late eighteenth and early nineteenth
centuries – a very broad and complex range of cultural developments associated with very large-scale and profound historical
changes. We couldn't hope to abstract from Romanticism (the
cultural movement) some precise term which would define a
particular literary form (romance); still less could we find in
Romanticism – which   includes   Byron's   *Don   Juan*   and
Wordsworth's *The Leech-gatherer* – some definite critical category
to pose *against* 'realism'.[3]

I think we can make use of Frye's distinction, but only by
accepting it as a suggestive indication that *Wuthering Heights* is a
complex novel which employs within itself widely differing
conventions. We should at the same time, in my view, resist any
attempt to assign the novel to some timeless *genre* of 'romance', or
to suggest that it does not properly belong with that complex and
comprehensive literary form we recognize by the term 'novel'.

In what follows I will be using the term 'romantic' to describe
certain characteristics of *Wuthering Heights* which relate it to *some*
familiar features of Romanticism – features that exhibit this
specific historical relationship, but which can be conveniently
assimilated to the common usage of 'romantic' (to describe a film,
an experience, a relationship). I am thinking of such things as the
use of dreams and the supernatural; the presence of fairy-tale and
folk-legend elements; and, above all, the emphasis on individual
sexual passion as a dominant though problematical value.[4] Such
effects are in contrast with more 'realistic' conventions –

conventions which endeavour to set the action of the novel on a solid basis of real human relations in an actual society; which establish a constant awareness of a real, everyday, social world and attempt to give a rationalistic explanation of all events and phenomena – and so on.

Both 'romantic' and 'realistic' then are used here in a consciously limited way (as they have to be if we are to use them at all), but with a definite and deliberate *historical* dimension. The presence of what I've called 'realism' in *Wuthering Heights* does not cut the novel off from Romanticism; nor does the presence of 'romantic' features take it outside the general form of the novel. If we tried to assert that a 'novel' can't contain 'romance', we would have to exclude Stendhal, Dickens and George Eliot from our category; if we sought a form of romance without realism we would have to exclude Malory.

Frye admits that 'pure examples of either form are never found ... the forms of prose fiction are mixed' (p. 305); and obviously *Wuthering Heights* is an example of just such a synthesis of conventions: the commonsense 'realist' perspective, in the form of Nelly Dean's narrative, is written into the novel along with strains of folk tale, ghost story and Gothic romance. I shall go on now to examine how some of these conventions are employed and synthesized in the style and structure of *Wuthering Heights*.

Folk tale

'See here, wife; I was never so beaten with anything in my life; but you must e'en take it as a gift of God, though it's as dark almost as if it came from the devil' (Ch. 4, p. 77). Mr Earnshaw's words could easily have come from a fairy story: he returns home from a journey and opens his coat to disclose not the expected gifts, but a human child – nameless, relationless, of mysterious origin. Heathcliff is either a gift from God or a dark emissary of the devil: the terms express his lack of social orientation and the duality of his nature, both promise and threat.

Mr Earnshaw's own *explanation* of where Heathcliff comes from is much more 'realistic'. Nelly says: '. . . all that I could make out ... was a tale of his seeing it starving, and houseless, and as good as dumb, in the streets of Liverpool where he picked it up and inquired for its owner – not a soul knew to whom it belonged' (Ch. 4, p. 78). 'Liverpool' – a real place, which lies outside the fictional world of Wuthering Heights, Thrushcross Grange and Gimmerton. Earnshaw offers a 'realistic' and therefore plausible and easily credible account of how, in practice, Heathcliff arrives at the Heights. What then is the relationship between these 'realistic' and 'fairy-tale' accounts of Heathcliff's origin?

They are not, obviously, incompatible or mutually exclusive. We should, I think, *believe* the realistic account, as far as it goes (there is no need to speculate about Heathcliff being Earnshaw's illegitimate child). This account tells us where Heathcliff came from and what he is, in so far as those 'facts' can be 'known' by the conventions of realism. But clearly those conventions do not tell us *enough* about what is happening here. The fairy-tale motif, then, played off against the 'realist' convention, enables the novelist to establish a much more complex understanding of Heathcliff's significance than either convention alone could provide. It is surely important to take the significance of *both* conventions, perceiving how they interact and enrich one another, rather than noticing one and ignoring the other.

Now read the following passage taken from Dorothy van Ghent's essay, and ask yourself whether she is giving a fair account of the incident discussed above when Heathcliff is brought home by Mr Earnshaw.

> Emily Brontë insists on Heathcliff's gypsy lack of origins, his lack of orientation and determination in the social world, his equivocal status on the edge of the human. When Mr Earnshaw first brings the child home, the child is an 'it', not a 'he', and 'dark almost as if it came from the devil'; and one of Nelly Dean's last reflections is, 'Is he a ghoul, or a vampire?' (p. 154)

DISCUSSION

Is Dorothy van Ghent really playing fair? She ignores the 'realistic' account of Heathcliff's provenance; she reduces the quotation 'You must e'en take it as a gift of God, though it's as dark almost as if it came from the devil' to the demonic reference alone; and if you look it up (Ch. 34, p. 359) you'll see that the passage in which Nelly thinks of Heathcliff as a 'ghoul or vampire' actually goes on to a naturalistic explanation which discredits the supernatural speculations.

I feel that Dorothy van Ghent is, in this particular instance, abstracting and simplifying, reducing the complexity of the novel in the interests of a single important emphasis. You may feel, of course, that the fairy-tale dimension is so important as to transcend or negate the 'realistic'. That is certainly not my view, but it is Dorothy van Ghent's, and her essay is a powerful and persuasive articulation of that view. I would want to insist that the 'realist' conventions should be taken as seriously as the 'romantic'. Whatever conclusions we come to about the problems posed here (and they are major ones – is Heathcliff human or supernatural? divine or diabolical?) we shall be unlikely to reach the right conclusions if we ignore a whole dimension of the novel.

Please study and make notes on the following passage from Chapter 7. How does this extract develop the fairy-tale motif?

> 'Oh, Heathcliff, you are showing a poor spirit! Come to the glass, and I'll let you see what you should wish. Do you mark those two lines between your eyes; and those thick brows, that instead of rising arched, sink in the middle; and that couple of black fiends, so deeply buried, who never open their windows boldly, but lurk glinting under them, like devil's spies? Wish and learn to smooth away the surly wrinkles, to raise your lids frankly, and change the fiends to confident, innocent angels, suspecting and doubting nothing, and always seeing friends where they are not sure of foes – Don't get the expression of a vicious cur that appears to know the kicks it gets are its desert, and yet hates all the world, as well as the kicker, for what it suffers.'
>
> 'In other words, I must wish for Edgar Linton's great blue eyes and even forehead', he replied. 'I do – and that won't help me to them.'
>
> 'A good heart will help you to a bonny face, my lad', I continued, 'if you were regular black; and a bad one will turn the bonniest into something worse than ugly. And now that we've done washing, and combing, and sulking – tell me whether you don't think yourself rather handsome? I'll tell you, I do. You're fit for a prince in disguise. Who knows, but your father was Emperor of China, and your mother an Indian queen, each of them able to buy up, with one week's income, Wuthering Heights and Thrushcross Grange together? And you were kidnapped by wicked sailors, and brought to England. Were I in your place, I would frame high notions of my birth; and the thoughts of what I was would give me courage and dignity to support the oppressions of a little farmer!' (Ch. 7, pp. 97–8)

DISCUSSION

The fairy-tale motif (which seems very much at home in Nelly's popular, 'folk' idiom) returns at this point, where Heathcliff, initially deeply offended by Catherine's behaviour on her return from Thrushcross Grange, has decided for her sake to accept some of the conventions of civilized social life: 'Nelly, make me decent, I'm going to be good' (Ch. 7, p. 96). As Nelly cleans him up, she offers him consolation for his real deprivation and forced inferiority: he should 'frame high notions' of his birth, believe that he is a prince in disguise, his father Emperor of China and his mother an Indian Queen. The images also, surely, offer a serious comment on Heathcliff's *value* as a human being – a value that can't be expressed in terms of title, status, wealth or property, but only in the imaginative richness of folk-tale myth and legend.

Heathcliff, however, has a strong sense that such images have a rather complex connection with a different order of 'reality' – the actual structure of social relationships that encompasses his real life. Nelly advises him to change his expression from the diabolical ('black fiends', 'devil's spies') to the angelic. Heathcliff's response is very perceptive: "'In other words, I must wish for Edgar Linton's great blue eyes and even forehead", he replied. "I do – and that won't help me to them"' (Ch. 7, p. 98).

Nelly's conventional religious symbolism in this specific situation, actually does reproduce the dominant social relationships of Heathcliff's society: the Lintons do have the blue eyes and fair hair, the stereotyped beauty of the conventional 'angel', while Heathcliff's dark appearance, his dirtiness and his resentful anger (the contrary of Edgar's 'confidence') make him seem 'demonic'. Heathcliff's point is that although he may be naturally and spiritually superior to Linton, that would not alter Linton's *social* advantages. The fairy-tale images then take on a *contradictory* relation to social reality: the infinite wealth of the legendary Emperors and Queens contrasts ironically with Heathcliff's real poverty, which he later turns to wealth – enough wealth in fact to 'buy up Wuthering Heights and Thrushcross Grange together' (Ch. 7, p. 98).

Again, realist and fairy-tale conventions interact with one another to express a complex and contradictory experience. Heathcliff *does* have human qualities which make him 'as good as' Edgar Linton: qualities that find their appropriate form of expression in fairy-tale mythology. But, at the same time, the realist conventions remind us that Linton possesses the real social advantages which Catherine chooses in preference to Heathcliff's *natural* virtues, his 'courage and dignity' (Ch. 7, p. 98). Immediately after this passage Heathcliff is exposed to a casual insult from the 'confident, innocent angel' (Ch. 7, p. 97) Edgar Linton, responds with violence and is brutally punished and forced into exclusion by Hindley Earnshaw. Heathcliff's spiritual virtues are forced by real social pressures into diabolical vindictiveness – the novel as a whole gives adequate expression to that complex process:

'I'm trying to settle how I shall pay Hindley back. I don't care how long I wait, if I can only do it, at last. I hope he will not die before I do'.

'For shame, Heathcliff!' said I. 'It is for God to punish wicked people; we should learn to forgive.'

'No, God won't have the satisfaction that I shall . . . ' (Ch. 7, p. 101)

Ghost story

Please re-read Chapter 3 of the novel.

I offered a detailed analysis of Lockwood's initial encounter with the Heights and its residents, stopping short of this very important passage dealing with Lockwood's dream. In a series of collisions and misunderstandings, Lockwood's judgement and perception are tested and proven defective. Finally, before he leaves the Heights for the Grange (where he will listen to the whole story from the beginning), Lockwood's capacity for 'knowing' himself and the world around him, his powers of understanding and judgement, are stretched to the utmost by an intense and terrifying encounter with the unknown.

Imagine for a moment that you have read Chapter 3 as a story printed by itself, without the context of the novel. A man has taken shelter from a snowstorm in an ancient, remote and mysterious house. He is put to bed in a structure resembling a coffin. He reads an intriguing old diary by the light of a candle, and falls asleep . . . to a terrifying dream . . . The narrative has all the makings of a ghost story, a real Victorian fireside 'chiller'; and it does not disappoint the reader's expectation, for it proves to be the preparation for a spectre's appearance. Before the ghost appears, however, Lockwood has another dream, of a very different character.

Compare Lockwood's two dreams (if the second one is a dream). Why do you think the novelist gives him two rather than one?

DISCUSSION

The clue to the first dream lies, I think, in Lockwood's words: 'Alas, for the effects of bad tea and bad temper! what else could it be that made me pass such a terrible night?' (Ch. 3, p. 64).

Lockwood's explanation of the dream, as a mental disturbance caused by a physical disorder, is entirely rational and 'realistic'. And the first dream invites explanation in such terms: both dreams derive their form and content from the diary Lockwood has been reading, but the first one does so much more directly, and is more easily explained by its source. In the first dream Lockwood takes the journey he really wants to take, to Thrushcross Grange, and the journey is again frustrated. He struggles with Joseph, recalling the old man's blocking his attempt to escape from the Heights. The comic parody of Joseph's Puritan idiom and behaviour is based on the diary's account of the 'awful Sunday' (Ch. 3, pp. 62–4). Lockwood's actual physical sensations intrude into the dream: 'Oh, how weary I grew. How I writhed, and yawned, and nodded, and revived!'(Ch. 3, p. 65); and the sound of the Rev. Jabes Branderham rapping on his pulpit proves to be the sound of a fir-branch tapping on the lattice. There is nothing improbable about this dream being engendered by entirely natural causes; and so it does nothing to shake Lockwood's normal rationality and common sense.

Then comes the real nightmare. It begins again with a 'real' experience, the sound of the fir-bough on the glass. But this time the dreamer, in the dream, is still in the oak-closet; so his knocking his hand through the glass has the effect of bringing 'normality' very sharply up against the unknown. This dream – though it originates in the diary's reference to separation between Catherine and Heathcliff – seems much more autonomous, external to Lockwood's own memories and physical sensations, as if it really *is* an apparition rather than a dream: '"Catherine Linton", it replied, shiveringly (why did I think of *Linton*? I had read *Earnshaw* twenty times for Linton)', (Ch. 3, p. 67).

The ghost-story convention is used then to build up in the reader an expectation which is initially denied (the first dream is only a dream, and hardly a disturbing one); and then fulfilled. A dream which is entirely explicable in 'realist' terms gives way to a dream in which the mind seems exposed to a genuinely super-natural order of reality.

Is Catherine's ghost really there, outside the window? The answer isn't quite as simple as it may appear to be. Once awake, Lockwood talks of ghosts and goblins; but for him the dream and 'real life' are obviously separate and mutually exclusive worlds. By the end of the novel he is still no believer in the supernatural. For Heathcliff, that separation of dream and reality does not exist: having heard Lockwood's account he, in full waking consciousness, throws open the window and cries his anguish out into the night.

Lockwood's comments are now rational and dismissive of the supernatural:

> I stood still, and was witness, involuntarily, to a piece of superstition on the part of my landlord, which belied, oddly, his apparent sense . . .
>   The spectre showed a spectre's ordinary caprice; it gave no sign of being . . . (Ch. 3, p. 70)

Lockwood interposes irony between himself and what he has just witnessed: for Heathcliff, the dream is perhaps more real than his waking life.

And yet the second dream has revealed to us something about Lockwood that certainly belies *his* apparent sense: 'Terror made me cruel; and, finding it useless to attempt shaking the creature off, I pulled its wrist onto the broken pane, and rubbed it to and fro till the blood ran down and soaked the bed clothes . . .' (Ch. 3, p. 67). How does such a disturbing access of violent cruelty arise in such a polite, gentlemanly, apparently rational individual? Evidently Lockwood's confrontation with what he doesn't know and cannot understand generates in him passions and sensations which seem alien to his character, but do in fact belong to it: as, in Freudian terms, dreams articulate, in disguised form, desires repressed by the conscious mind.

The narrative, then, by its synthesis of conventions, brings together 'realistic' dream and supernatural visitation, in order to explore the experience of a rational man brought to the very limits of his knowledge and understanding; and contrasts him with a man whose life discloses a constant interpenetration of natural and dream experience.

Please read the concluding pages of *Wuthering Heights*, Chapter 34, from 'The six men departed' (p. 365) to the end. How is the ghost-story convention used here?

DISCUSSION

Heathcliff is dead and buried; in normal terms that is the end of his story. And that is Lockwood's conclusion: he cannot comprehend how anyone could imagine 'unquiet slumbers, for the sleepers in that quiet earth' (Ch. 36, p. 367). But Nelly has offered some evidence to the contrary. None of it, we notice, is first-hand: *she* has seen nothing. In other words, the supernatural *reputation* of Catherine and Heathcliff lives in Nelly's mind in the form of popular folk tales and ghost stories. It is 'the country folks' who swear that Heathcliff *walks*: Joseph affirms that he has seen 'two on 'em', and the shepherd boy believes he has seen the spectres of Heathcliff and a woman. Nelly does not believe these accounts: 'He probably raised the phantoms from thinking, as he traversed the moors alone, on the nonsense he had heard his parents and companions repeat . . . I believe the dead are at peace'. On the other hand, a certain dubious fear testifies to the power these 'tales' exercise over her: 'Idle tales, you'll say, and so say I. Yet . . .'; 'I saw nothing; but . . .'; 'He probably raised the phantoms from thinking . . . yet still, I don't like being out in the dark . . .' Nelly's attitude is ambiguous: she does not want to believe these tales of the supernatural, but she acknowledges their power – and therefore perhaps, to some extent, their validity (Ch. 34, p. 366).

The reader is offered no less than three possible attitudes towards the dead. The country people not only believe that they 'walk', but *see* them. Lockwood is ironical about ghosts inhabiting the Heights, and his parting thoughts are of quiet and tranquillity (though what Lockwood 'imagines' is not necessarily the truth, and 'sleepers' could presumably awaken). Nelly mediates between these extremes: a country person herself, she also shares to an extent Lockwood's culture. Although she doesn't quite believe in the ghost stories, she does take them seriously – they have a serious *meaning*. 'I believe the dead are at peace, but it is not right to speak of them with levity', she says – which sounds like a mixture of sophisticated rationalism and folk superstition (Ch. 34, p. 366).

Does the reader have to make up his or her mind, to choose *one* of the proferred alternatives? Perhaps, but I think the alternatives are there to express the complexity and ambiguity of the experience presented. And I feel that my own reading of the novel resembles Nelly's account. Genuinely supernatural powers may have been invoked; but whether or not we acknowledge them as real, take them at their own valuation, is a matter for our own judgement. Nonetheless we must confess that the novel has touched such depths of human experience (and surely there is a long way to travel through human experience before we go *beyond* it) that it breaks the boundaries of the conventionally 'real', the familiarly 'known', the self-evidently and palpably 'true'. And this is why, right to the very end, 'romantic' conventions are constantly qualified, limited, criticized or supported by the conventions of 'realism'.

6. Second Generation

The continuation of the story into a second generation is prepared for from the very beginning of the novel. Lockwood meets Heathcliff, the second Catherine and Hareton simultaneously: he assumes that Catherine is Heathcliff's wife, that Hareton is Heathcliff's son; his reaction to Catherine junior mingles with his ideas about her mother. This confusion of the two generations produces a peculiar sense of overlap, which anticipates the extension of the story into the life of another, remarkably similar young couple. But the sequel is also a re-writing of the tragic tale of Catherine and Heathcliff; very similar conditions (social distinction, parental abuse, separation) produce an entirely different outcome: the younger couple manage to overcome the difficulties obstructing their relationship and achieve a harmonious and successful union.

Please read Chapters 32–34 of *Wuthering Heights*. How do you view the relationship of Catherine and Hareton as a sequel to the story of Catherine and Heathcliff? Is it a welcome and reassuring affirmation that love can defeat circumstances? Or a serious diminishing of interest and intensity, as the focus of the novel is deflected from the great tragic figures of Catherine and Heathcliff to their altogether smaller, more *ordinary* successors? Critics are naturally divided on this issue, so you may favour either point of view. The dominant view is probably that the sequel is a healing, therapeutic conclusion: a demonstration of the happiness that can come out of suffering, of the retorative power of love. Below I provide passages from two critics who take this view, and one from another critic who thinks the opposite. Compare their arguments and see what you think of them. Do you feel, as I do, that the third critic brings in an important emphasis that the first two ignore?

(a) *Wuthering Heights* is highly schematic and the demonstration of the corrective case-history of the second part is not just a matter of winding up the story and restoring the land to the legitimate heirs . . . having recognized Hareton's merits and her own needs, she [Catherine junior] freely chooses him as her husband, to become Catherine Earnshaw like her mother; but she has moved in the opposite direction from her mother who, born Catherine Earnshaw, became Catherine Linton of Thrushcross Grange . . . Cathy's mother had abandoned the degraded Heathcliff but her daughter generously takes the lad he had formed on that very pattern for revenge, thus righting the wrong.[1]

(b) We are left at the end with the fearful uncertainty of the fates of Catherine and Heathcliff, and with a sense of the costs to themselves and to others . . . of a love like theirs. Set against this is the certainty of the love which has sprung up between the second Catherine and Hareton and of the good it has already brought them. The last few chapters have a dual movement: as Heathcliff approaches death (and Catherine?) Hareton and the second Catherine approach each other . . . Catherine teaches Hareton and thus brings out the suppressed good in him; their wooing, as that of most of the protagonists in Charlotte Brontë's novels, is done in terms of the school-room . . . In the first pair, love was seen as a superhuman passion, as an affinity existing outside every social or moral category; in the second, the direction of the lovers' feelings is defined in the human and socially weighted word 'esteem' . . . ultimately, then, the novel affirms the domesticated virtues of man as a kind and social creature; it develops towards the Brontë version of the good life . . . which envisages an alleviation of suffering and loneliness through love that is kindness, affection, stronger teaching weaker, in a domesticated contex.[2]

(c) . . . the second-generation story is coming to its own conclusion and this 'coincidence' draws attention to the nature and degree of Emily Brontë's resolution of her conflict. At the last, within the space of a single page, we turn from the phantoms of Heathcliff and the elder Catherine restlessly walking the Heights in rain and thunder . . . to contemplate those other 'ramblers' on the moors, Hareton and the younger Catherine, who halt on the threshold of the old house to 'take a last look at the moon – or, more correctly, at each other by her light'. The closing passage of the book might suggest to an unwary reader that the final victory is to them. It is possible to mistake this last comment of Lockwood's, indicating 'calm' after 'storm', for a statement of calm's ultimate triumph. But such a reading

overlooks the departure of Hareton and the younger Catherine
to the valley, and their abandonment of the old house to the
spirits of the still restless Heathcliff and the elder Catherine.
There is, after all, no escape for Emily Brontë from her
emotional commitment to Heathcliff . . .[3]

DISCUSSION

The first two critics both argue that the novel (and the novelist)
endorses and approves the union of Catherine and Hareton, which
seems to resolve the problems and contradictions of the earlier
relationship, to synthesize the virtues of both Heights and Grange
cultures, and to draw a bitter and tragic story to a harmonious,
optimistic and reassuring conclusion. The third critic argues that
only an 'unwary' reader could come away with this impression: in
fact, the closing of the novel is more troubled and ambiguous, with
its emphasis on the continuing restless vitality of the ghosts. For this
critic the reassurances of the conclusion are not powerful enough to
efface the emotional intensity and tragic greatness of Heathcliff.
The point which this critic emphasizes and the others ignore, is the
question of narrative technique: for her the 'calm' of the ending is
imposed on it by Lockwood, and is not to be identified as Emily
Brontë's endorsement of the second generation.

   We should therefore, it seems to me, reconsider the sequel in
the light of the novel's narrative strategies. The end of Chapter 30
marks the end of Nelly Dean's story: the death of Linton Heathcliff
brings the narrative up to the point where the novel began, with
Lockwood's original visit to Wuthering Heights. When the
narrative resumes it is Lockwood giving an account of his revisiting
the Heights (in January of 1802) before returning to London. In
Chapter 32 he describes a journey North undertaken in September
of that year which leads him again to Wuthering Heights and to
Nelly's concluding narrative (Chapters 32–34).

   Please read Chapter 31. Compare this incident with
Lockwood's original visit. How does his function as *narrator*
compare here with the beginning of the novel? Consider the fact
that now Lockwood knows the story of Wuthering Heights, and is
no longer mystified by what he sees there. How does this affect his
relationship with the Heights and with the reader?

DISCUSSION

Lockwood has by now heard the whole story of the two families up
to the present date: so he is much more thoroughly informed about

the characters and the place which originally seemed to him so
inexplicably mysterious. But there is something odd about this re-
entry into the strange society which has been rendered by Nelly
Dean's narrative the subject of a story: almost indeed a legend,
located firmly in the past, its events and characters frequently
suggesting the archetypal simplicity of myth – the unquenchable
passion of the eternal lover, the implacable hatred of the great
avenger, and so on. Lockwood, although present in the opening
scenes as a character, has been constituted by Nelly's narrative as a
passive listener, an audience: akin not to the characters inside the
novel, but to the readers who, like ourselves, stand quite outside its
imaginative world. When Lockwood once again meets Catherine
and Hareton, he possesses the peculiarly privileged knowledge of a
reader of fiction: it is as if he suddenly finds himself transported
into the world of a book he's been reading:

> 'Mrs Heathcliff,' I said, after sitting some time mute, 'you are not
> aware that I am an acquaintance of yours? So intimate, that I think it
> strange you won't come and speak to me.' (Ch. 31, p. 331)

When Hareton is accused of robbing Catherine's library,
Lockwood has acquired from Nelly a prior knowledge of his
educational aspirations:

> 'Mr Hareton is desirous of increasing his amount of knowledge,' I
> said, coming to his rescue. 'He is not *envious* but *emulous* of your
> attainments – He'll be a clever scholar in a few years!' (p. 332)

And when Catherine parodies Hareton's stumbling attempts at
literacy, Lockwood is able to apply Nelly's sympathetic insights to
evaluate both Hareton's aspirations and Catherine's cruel mockery:

> The young man evidently thought it too bad that he should be
> laughed at for his ignorance, and then laughed at for trying to
> remove it. I had a similar notion, remembering Mrs. Dean's anecdote
> of his first attempt at enlightening the darkness in which he had been
> reared . . . (p. 332)

Consider again the effects of this shifting of narrative position.
Does it serve to make the narrative more understandable, or more
strange?

DISCUSSION

There are broadly two possible answers. Lockwood's narration is
always of the present (he writes in a kind of diary or journal style,
rarely more than a day away from the events he describes); while

Nelly's narrative is always of the past. It could be argued that one effect of Nelly's narrative is to distance events into a remote past, while a corresponding effect of Lockwood's is to draw them into a near and familiar present.

The events of the past can, of course, be either strange or apparently natural, and Nelly speaks of both kinds. The events of the present can be mysterious and terrifying, like Lockwood's dream; or the ordinary stuff of everyday life. Here, Lockwood is armed with the kind of knowledge that makes things intelligible: he makes no more mistakes about family relationships or dead rabbits. His knowledge brings the place and the people within the orbit of his, and our, understanding: a knowledge that naturalizes, familiarizes and domesticates.

The other type of answer is really the opposite of the first. We could argue that the effect of the narrative technique here is unsettling, suggesting as it does an unusual complexity in the relations between fiction and real life, between ourselves as readers and the imaginary world we are reading about. We don't normally walk into a situation equipped with the kind of inward acquaintance bestowed on us by fiction: especially when the people we are meeting, like characters in fiction, can have no inkling that we possess such knowledge. The writing here seems to be 'self-reflexive': that is, it draws the reader's attention to the mechanisms by which writing operates, making us aware of devices and techniques we normally take for granted and unconsciously accept. Instead of unselfconsciously *naturalizing* its vision of reality, making that vision seem a 'convincing' and 'realistic' representation; this writing seems to make its mechanisms unusually visible, making us think not just about 'life', but about the peculiar relationships created between life and the reader by literature.[4]

You might have been inclined either way on this question: because, it seems to me, both tendencies are present in the narrative. We have often previously noticed similar contrasts or contradictions: narative voices that familiarize, other voices that estrange; language that brings the novel close to earth, language that distance it into romance; conventions that insist on our comprehending events and personalities as real and intelligibly human, and conventions that render themselves and the experience they signify inexplicably and irreducibly strange. In the passage we are discussing there is one impulse or tendency consistent with the ideology of the narrator himself to *explain*: to account for everything in the belief that everything *can* be accounted for in naturalistic and rational terms. There is also another tendency, embodied primarily in the self-reflexive narrative, conveying the opposite suggestion – that any purely 'naturalistic' explanation of reality is bound to be inadequate.

At one level *Wuthering Heights* – through the commonsense of Nelly and the rationalism of Lockwood – insists on the natural reality and human relevance of its events and characters, right up to Lockwood's closing affirmation that the dead appear to be at peace. At another level – through the complexity of its narrative method and the inconsistency of its conventions – the novel insists that whatever reality is, it is not to be explained or appeased (like the unquiet ghosts of Catherine and Heathcliff) by the reassuring closures of fiction.

Please read Chapter 32. Then study and make notes on the following passage, considering these questions:

(1) What changes does Lockwood observe at Wuthering Heights?
(2) What is his position here in relation to Catherine and Hareton?
(3) How would you characterize the language of this passage?

I would have asked why Mrs Dean had deserted the Grange; but it was impossible to delay her at such a crisis, so I turned away and made my exit, rambling leisurely along, with the glow of a sinking sun behind, and the mild glory of a rising moon in front; one fading, and the other brightening, as I quitted the park, and climbed the stony by-road branching off to Mr Heathcliff's dwelling.

Before I arrived in sight of it, all that remained of day was a beamless, amber light along the west; but I could see every pebble on the path, and every blade of grass, by that splendid moon.

I had neither to climb the gate, nor to knock – it yielded to my hand.

That is an improvement! I thought. And I noticed another, by the aid of my nostrils; a fragrance of stocks and wall flowers, wafted on the air, from amongst the homely fruit trees.

Both doors and lattices were open; and, yet, as is usually the case in a coal district, a fine, red fire illumined the chimney; the comfort which the eye derives from it, renders the extra heat endurable. But the house of Wuthering Heights is so large, that the inmates have plenty of space for withdrawing out of its influence; and, accordingly, what inmates there were had stationed themselves not far from one of the windows. I could both see them and hear them talk before I entered, and looked and listened in consequence, being moved thereto by a mingled sense of curiosity, and envy that grew as I lingered.

'Con-*trary*!' said a voice, as sweet as a silver bell – That for the third time, you dunce! I'm not going to tell you, again – Recollect, or I pull your hair!'.

'Contrary, then,' answered another, in deep, but softened tones. 'And now, kiss me, for minding so well.'

'No, read it over first correctly, without a single mistake.'

The male speaker began to read – he was a young man, respectably dressed, and seated at a table, having a book before him. His handsome features glowed with pleasure, and his eyes kept impatiently wandering from the page to a small white hand over his shoulder, which recalled him by a smart slap on the cheek, whenever its owner detected such signs of inattention.

Its owner stood behind; her light shining ringlets blending at intervals, with his brown locks, as she bent to superintend his studies; and her face – it was lucky he could not see her face, or he would never have been so steady – I could, and I bit my lip, in spite, at having thrown away the chance I might have had, of doing something besides staring at its smiting beauty. (Ch. 32, pp. 337–8).

DISCUSSION

(1) The key-word is surely 'improvement'. What Lockwood means by improvement is abundantly clear: gates and doors previously locked are now open; flowers grow among the fruit trees. The cultural atmosphere of the house has moved away from the rough utilitarianism of the old farmstead, where a feudal defensiveness sought to exclude a hostile world, and where edible crops would always take priority over the unprofitable luxury of flowers. In a sense, the primitive culture of the Heights has moved closer to the sophisticated civilization of Thrushcross Grange.

(2) The same change is reflected in the relationship of Catherine and Hareton. Estrangement is replaced by friendship; conflict by sympathetic cooperation; anger and resentment by love. Witnessing that love, Lockwood reverts to his characteristic position of observer (if not *voyeur*): 'envious' of love, he steers clear of its manifestations in others. He avoids meeting Catherine and Hareton, and instead listens to their story through the medium of Nelly's narration: for him they are restored to their position as characters in fiction. Their reconciliation is effected on the common ground of literature: so here too the Heights and the Grange are synthesized in the persons of the two lovers.

(3) The language of the passage seems appropriate to the kind of fiction Lockwood is weaving around the lovers. It is best characterized as a kind of romance fiction: not, to be sure, the *genre* of 'romance' defined by Northrop Frye, but the more familiar medium of the popular romantic love-story.[5] Voices like silver bells, handsome features glowing with pleasure, small white hands, light shining ringlets, a face of smiting beauty: the language has all

the abstractness of conventional romance, in which every prince and every princess are the same as every other. The discourse is perhaps a sentimental adaptation of Lockwood's incorrigibly literary style of narration: he is bringing the story to a close appropriate to his own world-view. As we observed in the previous chapter, the testimony of the dialect-speaking shepherd-boy and Joseph propose a very different conclusion.

The story of Catherine and Heathcliff, a story of tragic conflict and *separation* by family enmity, class, marriage, death; was the necessary explanation of that perplexing scene of conflict and violence witnessed by Lockwood on his first visit to Wuthering Height. The narrative that follows this pasage (Chapters 32–4) serves to explain the scene of reconciliation between Catherine and Hareton, Heights and Grange. It is a story of hatred leading to love, conflict to mutual understanding, separation to union. It represents a distinct 'improvement' to Lockwood and a personal triumph for Nelly:

> . . . the crown of all my wishes will be the union of those two; I shall envy no one on their wedding-day – there won't be a happier woman than myself in England! (Ch. 32, p. 346)

We can pose our questions about the second generation in the terms used by the three critics quoted above: is the union of Catherine and Hareton affirmed by the novel as an unequivocal achievement, mending the failures of the tragic relations of Catherine and Heathcliff? Or is it rather a falling-off from the tragic intensity of the earlier story into the banality of a conventional vision of the Victorian 'good life'? But if we take into account the novel's narrative method, we raise a different set of questions: isn't the sequel a re-writing of the tragedy as 'romance', accomplished not by the novelist but by her narrators? Aren't Lockwood and Nelly the real authors of this fiction, while the novelist continually supplies evidence to dispute the consolatory calm of their conventional conclusion? The first kind of interpretation centres really on only one question: what was Emily Brontë's view of the second generation – a question that the novel persistently refuses to answer. The second kind of interpretation can raise in its wake other, more interesting questions: which do we prefer, the novel that settles and reconciles everything into the reassurance of a 'happy ending'; or the book that refuses to lay its ghosts, allowing them to return and trouble the precarious equilibrium of such an appeasement? For both novels are there, within the same set of covers.

7. Writer and Readers

1: *The novelist*

The Brontës' father, Patrick, was born Patrick O'Brunty or O'Prunty, the son of a peasant in Co. Down, Northern Ireland, in 1777. His home was a whitewashed shack some twenty feet square. Many Irishmen left their peasant homes to emigrate to England during this period, and went to work in the mills and factories of English cities, forming the poorest section of the slum population in towns like Manchester, Liverpool and London. Patrick was different: by 1802 (nobody knows how) he was at Cambridge University, where he took a degree and was ordained. He had a curacy in Yorkshire by 1809, married in 1812, and his wife bore their four literary children, Charlotte (1816), Branwell (1817), Emily Jane (1818), Anne (1820). There were also two older daughters, who died young. The Rev. Patrick was appointed to the incumbency of Haworth in Yorkshire in 1820; he had risen rapidly from a barefoot Irish peasant to a respectable Anglican clergyman.

Patrick Brontë's wife died in 1822, when Emily was only four years old. In 1824 she was sent to join her sisters at the Clergy Daughters' school, Cowan Bridge (the 'Lowood School' of Charlotte Brontës *Jane Eyre*). Her two elder sisters Maria and Elizabeth returned home to die in early 1825, and when the school suffered a typhoid epidemic later in that year, the other children were withdrawn. At home the children enjoyed a very active and intense play-life which very soon was extended into writing. Branwell and Charlotte began a vogue for the writing of fiction and poetry which persisted for all four into adulthood, beginning with fantasy romances about a fabulous kingdom ('Glasstown')

populated by romance monarchs and historical characters such as
the Duke of Wellington. From 1872 the children were writing
plays; and when Charlotte was again sent away to school in 1831,
Emily and Anne founded their imaginary kingdom of 'Gondal'. The
very interesting interpenetration of fantasy and reality apparently
typical of their home-life, can be seen in one of Emily's 'diary-
papers', written in 1834:

> I fed Rainbow, Diamond, Snowflake Jasper Pheasant (alias) this
> morning Branwell went down to Mr Driver's and brought news that
> Sir Robert Peel was going to be invited to stand for Leeds   Anne and
> I have been peeling apples for Charlotte to make us an apple pudding
> and for Aunt nuts and apples   Charlotte said she made puddings
> perfectly and she was a quick but limited intellect. Tabby said just
> now Come Anne pilloputate (i.e. pill a potato) Aunt has come into
> the kitchen just now and said where are your feet Anne   Anne
> answered on the floor Aunt   papa opened the parlour door and
> gave Branwell a letter saying here Branwell read this and show it to
> your Aunt and Charlotte – the Gondals are discovering the interior
> of Gaaldine   Sally Mosley is washing in the back kitchen [1]

('Aunt' was Maria Branwell, their mother's elder sister, who moved
in after Mrs Brontë's death. 'Tabby' is Tabitha Aykroyd, family
servant).

Emily went again to school in 1835, this time to Miss Wooler's
school at Roe Head. Her biographers have suggested that Emily
found school life intolerably inconducive after the liberty of home,
and was for the first time forced back into inner resources of
fantasy and self-communing. Within three months she had fallen ill
and returned home. The following two years she spent at home,
and seems to have become at this time close to her brother
Branwell. In 1837 she went to a school in Halifax as a teacher, and
wrote some remarkable poems describing forms of mystical
experience. She accompanied Charlotte to Brussels in 1842,
returning when their aunt died later in the year. Charlotte returned
to Brussels, Emily remained at home.

It was Charlotte's discovery, after her return home in 1844, of
some of Emily's poems that encouraged her to seek publication for
some of the family's literary productions. A volume of verse by the
three sisters come out in 1846. This was followed by the
publication in 1847 of three novels, Charlotte's *Jane Eyre*, Anne's
Agnes Grey, and Emily's *Wuthering Heights*: published under
pseudonyms – Currer, Acton and Ellis Bell – designed to appear
not distinctly male, but at any rate to disguise the authors' female
identities. Emily died of tuberculosis in 1849.

"Haworth Parsonage" (photo: David Sheppard)

V. R.

BY THE QUEEN.
A
PROCLAMATION.

VICTORIA R.

WHEREAS

Great Numbers of evil-disposed and disorderly Persons have lately, in some Parts of GREAT BRITAIN, assembled themselves together after Sun-set, by Torch-light, in large Bodies and in a tumultuous Manner, with Banners, Flags, and other Ensigns, and have continued so assembled until a late Hour of the Night, and during the Time they were so assembled have, by loud Shouts and Noises, and by the Discharge of Fire-Arms, and the Display of Weapons of Offence, greatly alarmed the Inhabitants of the Neighbourhood of such Assemblies, and endangered the Public Peace: WE, therefore, being sensible of the mischievous Consequences to be apprehended from such illegal Meetings, and of the dangerous Tendency thereof, not only to the Peace of Our Kingdom, but to the Lives and Properties of Our Subjects, do hereby warn and command all Persons to desist from such Assemblies at their Peril; and do further command all Justices of Peace, Sheriffs, Constables, and other Peace Officers to use their utmost Endeavours to prevent all such illegal Assemblies, and to bring the Offenders to Justice.

Given at our Court at WINDSOR, this Twelfth Day of DECEMBER, in the Year Eighteen Hundred and Thirty-eight, and in the Second Year of our Reign.

GOD SAVE THE QUEEN.

W. H. BLACKBURN, PRINTER, 44, MARKET-STREET, BRADFORD.

"Proclamation, 1838 (Haworth Parsonage Museum)."

Emily Brontë's personality is not easy to define: she was far less forthcoming and desirous of celebrity than her sister Charlotte; though Charlotte's fame came in any case after Emily's death. The impression that has been conveyed by the few facts and reminiscences of her life is of a woman remarkably reserved and self-sufficient; highly intellectual yet apparently contented with a retired domestic life; self-willed but loyal, sardonic but generous. Charlotte Brontë's friend Ellen Nussey described Emily as 'intensely loveable' yet commanding respect, even awe – she invited confidence in her moral power'.[2] She seems to have valued her creative powers very highly, even seeing them as the visitations of a kind of deity; yet she apparently consented reluctantly to having her writings published. She strikes me as a writer who was equally at home in the private worlds of fantasy and in the everyday world of human behaviour; a conscious and disciplined artist, as well as an imaginative genius.

One by-product of the unusual tenor of her life has been a tendency to protray her as a weird, isolated genius, communing only with nature and her own imagination, divorced from human society and the intercourse of other human beings. It is perhaps worth pointing out that Haworth was not the remote and isolated country village which figures in the 'Brontë legend'. It was a big village near Keighley, in the industrial West Riding of Yorkshire, near the centre of the woollen area: a rapidly growing town, whose population between 1811 and 1831 went from 3,971 to 5,835. There was nothing 'out of touch' about Haworth Parsonage; there couldn't possibly have been, since one of the most rapidly developing areas of industrial England was on its doorstep. The children inherited their father's interest in politics and spent much time in political discussion. When the *Leeds Mercury* printed a series of letters from Richard Oastler about child labour in the worsted mills, the paper went to the Parsonage and Charlotte may have read it. In any case, when she came to write about factories in her novel *Shirley* she didn't have to go as far as Bradford for material – there were worsted mills in Haworth as well.

The Brontës grew up in the second, and in many ways the most important, phase of the industrial revolution. It was not the age of the primary inventions, of the first introduction of power-driven machinery and of the factory system, but rather of the consolidation and victory of that system, of the development of full-scale capitalism with its accompanying cycle of boom and slump and of continuous and intense class-conflict. Early in the century came the Luddite riots; there followed in succession the Radical agitation of the Peterloo period, the struggle around the Reform Bill of 1832, the growth of Trade Unionism in the early thirties, the fight for improved factory conditions and against the Poor Law of 1834, and finally the Chartist movement from 1838 to 1848. In every one of these, the West-Riding was a storm-centre.[3]

These events were too close to be missed or ignored: Patrick Brontë was, as a clergyman, actually involved in strikes, and lock-outs, at one time incurring the wrath of the local 'ratepayers' by assisting the locked-out workers of his parish. Charlotte and Emily weren't confined to Haworth, but went much to Bradford, Keighley and Leeds – and for a short time to Brussels; they both went to a school at Halifax, a Chartist stronghold, and the scene of one of the most notable Poor Law riots. On Hartshead Moor, only a few miles away, one of the biggest Chartist torchlight rallies took place in 1838. Charlotte used her experience of these events in her novel *Shirley*: Emily didn't write about them directly, but none the less they constitute her milieu, her social world.

I have been insisting on the connections between Emily Brontë's life and the historical world in which she wrote because it seems to me necessary to challenge the much more dominant conventional view which emphasizes her isolation, individuality and eccentric genius. It would however be very wrong to leave you with the impression that the Brontës could be comfortably assimilated as normal or typical figures in mid-nineteenth-century Britain. The very *unusual* character of their personal lives has to be taken in the context of their evident absorption into their real historical context. Terry Eagleton has written brilliantly about this peculiar synthesis of the typical and the eccentric, the representative and the unique; and I should like to leave you to reflect on a passage from his book *Myths of Power*:

The Brontës lived through an era of disruptive social change, and lived that disruption at a peculiarly vulnerable point. Far from being sublimely secluded from their history, that history entered, shaped and violated the inmost recesses of their personal lives ... Their situation is unique, certainly – but unique in its classical condensing of an unusually wide range of historical tensions. They happened to live in a region which revealed the friction between land and industry in peculiarly stark form – starker, certainly, than in a purely agrarian or industrial area. The same part of the country ... witnessed working-class struggle at an extraordinary pitch of militancy, and in that sense too highlighted certain 'typical' historical trends. These pervasive social conflicts were then peculiarly intensified by the sisters' personal situation. They were, to begin with, placed at a painfully ambiguous point in the social structure, as the daughters of a clergyman with the inferior status of 'perpetual curate' who had thrust his way up from poverty; they strove as a family to maintain reasonably 'genteel' standards in a traditionally rough-and-ready environment. They were, moreover, socially insecure *women* – members of a cruelly oppressed group whose victimized condition reflected a more widespread exploitation. And they were *educated* women, trapped in an almost intolerable deadlock between culture and economics – between imaginative aspiration and the cold truth of a society which could use them merely as 'higher' servants. They were *isolated* educated women, socially and geographically remote from a world with which they nonetheless maintained close intellectual touch, and so driven back on themselves in solitary emotional hungering. At certain points in their fiction, indeed, that loneliness becomes type and image of the isolation of all men in an individualist society. And as if this were not enough, they were forced to endure in their childhood an especially brutal form of ideological oppression – Calvinism.

In the unique imaginative formation of the Brontës, then, social, sexual, cultural, religious and geographical issues fuse into an overdetermined unity. It is for this reason that we can trace in their very 'eccentricity' the contours of a common condition, detect in their highly specific life-style the unfolding of a general grammar. In a society where banishment from a centre seemed a general experience, the Brontës' 'eccentric' situation begins to seem curiously typical. (pp. 7–9).

2: Reception

Throughout the first half of the nineteenth century the novel was growing in status as a literary form: from being regarded as primarily entertainment, it was coming to be regarded as something like a serious art-form. Kathleen Tillotson in *Novels of the Eighteen-Forties* has shown that this growth in respectability can be seen in the literary journals of the time: in the 1840s the style of novel-reviewing gradually changed from the unambitious kind of review which simply printed long passages from the book under consideration, possibly praising it as a 'good story', to more general considerations of the novel as an art-form. Of course critics had taken novels seriously before, but there were no general assumptions to that effect among readers. When Sir Walter Scott reviewed Jane Austen's *Emma* he was fully aware of the value of what he had before him, but nevertheless felt it necessary to insist that the novel was *not* 'beneath the sober consideration of a critic'.[4]

But what sort of 'seriousness' would be expected of a novel in the 1840s by readers and reviewers? Look for a moment at two short pieces: from Daniel Defoe's *Colonel Jack* and from Samuel

Richardson's *Clarissa*. How do these writers justify the 'seriousness' of their productions?

> Every wicked reader will here be encouraged to change, and it will appear that the best and only good end of a wicked misspent life is repentance; that in this, there is comfort, peace, and often-times hope, and that the penitent shall be returned like the prodigal, *and his latter end be better than his beginning*.
>
> While these things, and such as these, are the ends and designs of the whole book, I think I need not say one word more as an apology for any part of the rest, no, nor for the whole; if discouraging everything that is evil, and encouraging everything that is virtuous and good; I say, if these appear to be the whole scope and design of the publishing this story, no objection can lie against it, neither it is of the least moment to inquire whether the colonel hath told his own story true or not; if he has made it a history or a parable, it will be equally useful, and capable of doing good; and in that it recommends itself without any other introduction.[5]

> In the general depravity, when even the pulpit has lost great part of its weight, and the clergy are considered as a body of interested men, the author thought he should be able to answer it to his own heart, be the success what it would, if he threw in his mite towards introducing a reformation so much wanted: and he imagined, that if an age given up to diversion and entertainment, he could steal in, as may be said, and investigate the great doctrines of Christianity under the fashionable guise of an amusement, he should be most likely to serve his purpose; remembering that of the poet:

> 'A verse may find him who a sermon flies,
> And turn delight into a sacrifice . . .'[6]

DISCUSSION

They justify their 'seriousness' by insisting that novels are really didactic, that they celebrate or exemplify principles of orthodox morality, and that they have a beneficial effect on the moral sensibility of the reader.

Now look at this passage from Henry James's Preface to *Portrait of a Lady*. What differences of approach strike you between Defoe and James?

> . . . the one measure of the worth of a given subject, the question about it that, rightly answered, disposes of all others – is it valid, in a word is it genuine, is it sincere, the result of some direct impression or perception of life? . . . There is, I think, no more nutritive or suggestive truth in this connexion than that of the perfect depend-

ence of the 'moral' sense of a work of art on the amount of felt life concerned in producing it. The question comes back thus, obviously, to the kind and degree of the artist's prime sensibility, which is the soil out of which his subject springs. The quality and capacity of that soil, its ability to 'grow' with due freshness and straightness any vision of life, represents, strongly or weakly, the projected morality. That element is but another name for the more or less close connexion of the subject with some mark made on the intelligence, with some sincere experience.[7]

DISCUSSION

Defoe thinks it's more important for a novel to be 'moral' than to be 'true'. Whether Colonel Jack's story is true or not doesn't matter, as long as the effect of the story is not immoral – as long as virtue is seen to be rewarded and vice punished. Henry James thinks the opposite: 'the question about it that ... disposes of all others – is it valid, in a word is it genuine, is it sincere, the result of some direct impression or perception of life? ... ' and he talks about 'the perfect dependence of the "moral" sense of a work of art on the amount of felt life concerned in producing it'. The novel's faithful representation of life is more important to James than its moral orthodoxy.

I wouldn't like to mislead you about these eighteenth-century novelists, who weren't by any means as simple-minded as this might suggest. In both these quotations, they are (I think) having their readers on – since the novels themselves aren't really moral tracts at all. Still, the fact that they could talk about (and play upon) these general attitudes indicates that they existed: and they are what we are concerned with here.

Two hundred years or so separate Defoe from James, two hundred years of social, literary and human change, during which time novels justified themselves as art to readers and critics alike. But one can see from the reviews of *Wuthering Heights* that the belief in the novel as didactic fiction was still going strong in the 1840s and 1850s. Critics and reviewers were divided about *Wuthering Heights*: some saw it as a radically immoral book; others saw it in terms of orthodox Christian or conventional morality, arguing that Heathcliff is presented clearly by Emily Brontë for our moral judgement and inevitable moral repudiation. Notice that whichever view they hold, critics were generally agreed about what the moral character and function of the novel ought to be.[8]

This novel contains, undoubtedly, powerful writing, and yet it seems to be thrown away. We want to know the object of a fiction. Once people were content with a crude collection of mysteries. Now they desire to know why the mysteries are revealed. Do they teach mankind to avoid one course and take another? Do they dissect any portion of existing society, exhibiting together its weak and strong points? If these questions were asked regarding *Wuthering Heights* there could not be an affirmative answer given. (*Tate's Edinburgh Magazine*, February 1848)

What may be the moral which the author wished the reader to deduce from the work it is difficult to say, and we refrain from assigning any, because, to speak honestly, we have discovered none ... There seems to us great power in the book, but it is a purposeless power. (*Douglas Jerrold's Weekly Newspaper*, 15 January 1848)

These critics felt that *Wuthering Heights* was immoral; others found it morally satisfactory.

Heathcliff ... is an incarnation of evil qualities; implacable hate, ingratitude, cruelty, falsehood, selfishness, and revenge ... If this book be the first work of its author, we hope that he will produce a second ... looking steadily at human life, under all its moods, for those pictures of the passions that he may desire to sketch for our public benefit. (*Examiner*, 8 January 1848)

If the book have any moral it serves to show how fierce, how inhuman a passion personal attachment to another may become, and how reckless of the welfare of its object. (*National Review*, July 1857)

The story shows the brutalizing influence of unchecked passion. His characters are a commentary on the truth that there is no tyranny in the world like that which thoughts of evil exercise in the daring and reckless breast. (*Britannia*, 15 January 1848)

Charlotte Brontë was, characteristically, divided on this issue:[9]

Whether it is right or advisable to create beings like Heathcliff I do not know: I scarcely think it is. But this I know: the writer who possesses the creative gift owns something of which he is not always master – something that at times strangely wills and works for itself. He may lay down rules and principles, and to rules and principles it will perhaps for years lie in subjection; and then, haply without any warning of revolt, there comes a time when it will no longer consent to 'harrow the vallies, or be bound with a band in the furrow ...'

Heathcliff, indeed, stands unredeemed; never once swerving in his arrow-straight course to perdition ...

Generally the novels of Charlotte and Anne were found more palatable because they could be fitted easily into the category of didactic fiction. *Agnes Grey* was said to have 'an advantage over its predecessor [i.e. *Wuthering Heights*], that while its language is less ambitious and less repulsive, it fills the mind with a lasting picture of love and happiness succeeding to scorn and affliction, and teaches us to put every trust in a supreme wisdom and goodness' (*New Monthly Magazine*, 52, January 1848). Even *Jane Eyre* could be seen by a ladies' magazine, *La Belle Assemblée* as 'a warning to all placed in authority over the young, whether in the capacity of parent, teacher or nurse . . . a warning against leaving the young and impressible to the charge of uneducated and lax-principled servants'.[10] But at least one reviewer, Elizabeth Rigby in the *Quarterly Review* for December 1848, lumped both *Jane Eyre* and *Wuthering Heights* together and went much further than a diagnosis of unprincipled morality:[11]

> Altogether the autobiography of *Jane Eyre* is a pre-eminently anti-Christian composition. There is throughout it a murmuring against the comforts of the rich and privations of the poor, which, as far as each individual is concerned, is a murmuring against God's appointment – there is a proud and perpetual assertion of the rights of man, for which we find no authority in either God's word or God's providence – there is that pervading tone of ungodly discontent which is at once the most prominent and the most subtle evil which the law and the pulpit, which all civilized society in fact has at the present day to contend with. We do not hesitate to say that the tone of mind and thought which has overthrown authority and violated every code human and divine abroad, and has fostered Chartism and rebellion at home, is the same which has also written *Jane Eyre*.

Wuthering Heights was even worse: 'too odiously and abominably pagan to appeal to the most vitiated class of English readers'. 1848 was a 'year of revolutions:' the February Revolution which overthrew the constitutional monarchy in France; revolutions all over Europe – in Italy, Hungary, South Germany; the crisis of Chartism in England; the publication of the *Manifesto of the Communist Party* by Marx and Engels. The reviewer's tone is clearly exaggerated, and extremely reactionary. But it seems to me interesting that a respected and influential review should have detected in the Brontë novels some of that 'revolutionary' spirit and feeling. The charges point at least to the very disturbed and changing world in which the novels are written; and perhaps also to the nature of the relationship between those novels and that world of history.

Contemporary criticism

Most of the criticism you have been introduced to in this *Guide* is
traditional 'interpretative' criticism of one school or another: most
of the critics I have quoted start from the assumption that we can
reach the best understanding of a literary text by attending to
certain aspects of its form, or by installing it into a particular
historical, theoretical or philosophical context. Some of the most
recent forms of criticism are much more concerned to acknowledge
the 'plurality' of literature: that is, the presence or potentiality for
many meanings within a single literary text. Most literary criticism
has admitted that texts can look rather different when seen from
different angles, even though the text is held to possess a fixed,
intrinsic meaning. Post-structuralist criticism however maintains
that the meaning of a text actually changes from one group of
readers to another: the meaning of a text is never *inside* it, but is
constructed differently as it is read, interpreted, set into relationships with other texts, by different readers in different times and
places.

Let us take as an example of traditional criticism an essay I
have already quoted, 'A Fresh Approach to *Wuthering Heights*', by
Q.D. Leavis. That essay is discussed and criticized by Frank
Kermode in his book *The Classic*: the conflict of these two
approaches can illustrate for us the differences between traditional
and post-structuralist literary criticism.[12]

Mrs Leavis' argument is that *Wuthering Heights* is a mixture
of successful and unsuccessful elements: at the heart of the novel
there is a parable about the importance of 'maturity' in human
relationships, based on the contrast between the first Catherine
who permits her passions to destroy her, and the second Catherine
who achieves a 'mature' and viable relationship with Hareton
Earnshaw. Much of what remains in the novel Mrs Leavis finds
unsatisfactory, and speculates that most of it is the result of Emily
Brontë's incorporation into the novel of crude and undigested
material from earlier writing projects. Heathcliff, in Mrs Leavis'
view, is the unrealized focus of several different artistic impulses,
and should therefore be excluded from our critical concentration
on the 'real' meaning of the novel. It is clear from this summary that
Mrs Leavis' method involves an insistence that some parts of the
novel are important, others not; so that any interpretation which
concerned itself with the parts she rejects would inevitably be
wrong. Her essay thus *privileges* some parts of the novel over
others, and one interpretation over any possible alternative. Her

critical method produces for us a 'closed' text.

The essay by Frank Kermode already mentioned is an instance of post-structuralist criticism: it offers an interpretation of *Wuthering Heights* (involving a complex patterning of the names *Earnshaw, Heathcliff* and *Linton*); but an interpretation which acknowledges the text's plurality. It also insists that what it proposes has no finality or absoluteness, but is merely a selective reading of certain aspects of the novel. Kermode points out that the enormously wide variety of interpretations to which this novel has been subjected, is in practice a response to something in the nature of the novel itself, and the real reason why it is a 'classic': however many readers and critics attempt to 'close' the novel, the novel keeps opening itself up again. Without that potentiality for plurality of meaning, the novel would not be able to survive beyond its own historical and cultural context. Kermode's reading is designed to 'open' rather than 'close': to acknowledge plurality, to admit variety of interpretations, to make reading a matter of *liberty*, rather than the submission to *authority*.

Such an approach involves difficulties too. Can a text become the centre of an *infinite* variety of interpretations, all equally valid? Suppose some of them have nothing to do with the text, and appear entirely unconvincing in their arguments? Kermode suggests that there is a minimum level of 'competance' required of a reader before an interpretation can be regarded as valid: the reader has to know certain facts, be aware of previous criticism, be familiar with certain methods and approaches, before *anything* meaningful can be said about the text in question. I would argue myself that some criterion of *relevance* must be involved too: the text *does* have a specific form, which can sanction some interpretations and not others. We could imagine an interpretation of *Wuthering Heights* which proposed that Heathcliff was really the devil; but if someone were to argue that Nelly Dean is the devil we wouldn't attach any importance to their point of view.

Nonetheless, it is my own conviction that post-structuralist criticism has produced some remarkable results in its revolutionizing of traditional critical methods, and that its impact on literary studies cannot be ignored. As an illustration of what such criticism can do with a classic text, I would recommend that you read a brilliant though difficult essay by David Musselwhite on *Wuthering Heights*. The essay may be difficult to obtain, so I have provided a summary of its argument here.[13]

Following the French theorists Pierre Macherey and Etienne Balibar, Musselwhite proceeds from the assumption that 'literature is an institutional practice designed to produce consensus, to guarantee and perpetuate an ideological hegemony' (p. 3): that is, the function of literature is to maintain the *status quo* in a society by taking that society's contradictions and resolving them into myths of harmony and reconciliation. A novel may deal with poverty, unemployment, social injustice, oppression: but its real purpose is not to *attack* those evils and remove them (a *political* activity), but to give the reader an illusory experience of social reconciliation which will make such evils seem tolerable or unavoidable: 'Is not literature an ideological "opérateur", designed to ingest the unacceptable and regurgitate it as the acceptable?' (p. 3). For this approach, that which is at the centre of a novel is an ideological mystification: and if we want to discover what the novel can tell us about reality, we should be examining not its harmony and completeness, but its cracks and contradictions, the rough edges where it has not quite succeeded in transforming the 'unacceptable' difficulties of reality into the 'acceptable' harmony of literature. Musselwhite finds in *Wuthering Heights* an image which directly supports his approach: he notes that when Lockwood finds Catherine's Bible (in Chapter 3) he does not read the text itself, but looks at what is written on its margins, the girl's scribbled diary-paper which 'defaces' the text itself. Pursuing what is on the *fringes* of the book leads Lockwood to his encounter with the unknown, the 'Other' which for Musselwhite is the reality literature exists to conceal: 'It is the marginalia of an injured tome that fascinates him, not the immaculate positivity of the printed word. Pursuing the marginal, the interstitial, the intercalcated and the injured text one is led to the pathos and the passion, the horror and the dread of the Other' (p. 3). Musselwhite notes that when Catherine's ghost tries to break in through the window, Lockwood protects himself against the incursion by erecting a pile of *books*: 'It is this closure, this shutting out of the Other, by erecting a pile of books that is the real tragedy of the novel' (p. 4). Like literature, Lockwood denies the true nature of reality by constructing a defensive barrier against its irruptions. The image of the book as an agent of reconciliation reappears with the second stage of the story, the union of Catherine Heathcliff and Hareton Earnshaw which is clearly a replaying (in Musselwhite's terms, a *rewriting*) of the tragic story of Catherine and Heathcliff. The second pair of lovers is witnessed by Lockwood uniting in the act of *reading*: 'the Book has been re-established' (p. 5). The novel doesn't, according to Musselwhite, *endorse* this reconciliation, this 'closure': *Wuthering Heights* is very different from the book they are reading, since *that* can only function as an agent of reconciliation; while *Wuthering Heights* can expose and reveal how literature functions as a mode of ideological resolution, without ceasing to be literature in its own right.

Musselwhite's essay has all the brilliance and all the difficulty of this school of criticism: sometimes startlingly illuminating, sometimes self-indulgently ingenious. It seems to me that neither this essay, nor the essay by Frank Kermode discussed earlier, can justly be accused (as such criticism is most frequently accused) of developing theoretical interests *at the expense* of a work of literature: of failing to respond to its unique and specific qualities, its individual identity. I think you'll agree that both essays are deeply responsive to some qualities in the nature of this complex novel.

The other recent source of original and illuminating work on the Brontës is feminist criticism. There has always been a natural interest in the Brontë sisters among women – the unusual phenomenon of a *sorority* of three talented writers (with a talented brother who failed to achieve anything) inevitably draws the interest of female readers and critics. Thus most of the Brontë biographers have been women: and there have been admirable attempts to address the problems of female authorship in books such as Inga-Stina Ewbank's *Their Proper Sphere*.

Contemporary feminist criticism tends to be more overtly part of the wider movement for female emancipation; of the general effort to assert a feminist consciousness or philosophy into culture and society. Such criticism tends to be more overtly political, declaring its ideological purposes openly: it therefore goes beyond the reinterpretation of texts, to require of its readers a radical critique of the whole concept of literature, and of the institutions which support literature as a cultural activity. For feminists, these institutions are male-dominated, both in terms of the men who run them, and the 'patriarchal' ideologies they presuppose and foster. A useful example of this project is Joanna Russ' *How to Suppress Womens' Writing*, which argues that male-dominated literary establishments employ various strategies to deal with womens' writing without ever acknowledging it on equal terms. [14] She shows, for example, that several critics responded to *Wuthering Heights* (by Ellis Bell) as a work of gloomy and oppressive but *powerful* imagination; of exaggerated and partial but *accurate* imitation of life. Once reviewers learned in 1850 that Ellis Bell was a woman, their attitude abruptly changed: now the novel became the work of an isolated and hungry *fantasy*, the expression of powerful subjective emotions rather than a portrayal of the darker side of life. It can be seen that these reviewers reacted quite differently to the novel on the basis of their assumption about the author's sex: they found initially in the novel *experience* and *power*, neither of which a Victorian woman should really possess. Once they knew she was a woman, they denied her both qualities.

Other feminist critics have sought to 'recover' female writing from the kind of masculine versions of history and culture into which it has been 'processed': to see female writers not as the accessories of a male-dominated tradition, but as the articulators of a unique and specific female experience of life. The title of Elaine Showalter's *A Literature of Their Own* summarizes that feminist ambition.[15] In practice this means re-reading classic texts to emphasize the 'female' elements. A feminist critic, for example, would give to Catherine Earnshaw the kind of attention I have given to Heathcliff. I have already quoted Patricia Meyer Spacks' interpretation, which reduces Heathcliff to the product of Catherine's fantasy. A similar treatment can be found in Sandra Gilbert and Susan Gubar's *The Madwoman in the Attic*: this very elaborate and learned argument proposes that *Wuthering Heights* should be linked with writers like Milton and Blake, who both portrayed visions of 'Hell' as a symbolic focus of enormous energy and power. Blake consciously reversed the conventional distinction between heaven and hell, and defined Hell as 'Energy' and 'Eternal Delight'. Gilbert and Gubar argue that initially Catherine occupies a state of feminist liberty akin to Blake's Hell: her power is exercised through her instrument Heathcliff, who is simply an extension of her female will. Her history is that of an inverted 'fall' into patriarchal society, symbolized by Edgar Linton and Thrushcross Grange, an environment in which she cannot survive. Her daughter finally makes her peace with patriarchy, and we are left with a mythical memory of feminine freedom and power.[16]

It would be unfair to engage in critical discussion with arguments whose outlines I have barely sketched: if you are interested in pursuing the questions raised by such feminist interventions, it will be necessary for you to follow my references to their sources. You might wish to discover whether these feminist critics make a convincing case for their subordination of Heathcliff to Catherine: isn't he in some respects stubbornly independent of her (when he leaves Wuthering Heights half-way through Catherine's speech to Nelly in Chapter 9)? Or you might feel that in interpreting the book entirely on the symbolic and mythical level, the authors of *The Madwoman in the Attic* are ignoring important constitutive features of the novel, such as its narrative method and its 'realist' basis?

It is fitting that I should end with questions, as the novel itself does so. Like *Wuthering Heights*, this *Guide* does not propose to end with an answer: if it has done its job, its question should be reaching out beyond its perimeters as Catherine reaches to Heathcliff from beyond the grave. The blank space below my final words is not an emptiness, but a space to be filled with you own activity of thought and feeling. Whatever we 'close', we leave something significant out in the 'open'; and that is as true of this book as it is of the novel it has sought, in collaboration with you, to interpret.

Notes

Chapter One: Narrative (pp. 1–13)
1   Charlotte Brontë: 'Biographical Notice of Ellis and Acton Bell' (1850).
    See David Daiches (ed.) Emily Brontë, *Wuthering Heights* (Penguin English Library: 1965), p. 33. All page references to the text are to this edition of the novel.
2   Charlotte Brontë: 'Editor's Preface to the New Edition of *Wuthering Heights*' (1850). As above edition, *Wuthering Heights*, p. 40.
3   Frank Kermode: *The Classic* (Faber: 1975), p. 121.
4   Thomas A. Vogler: 'Introduction' to his edition *Twenteith-century Interpretations of Wuthering Heights*, (Prentice-Hall: 1968), p. 5.
5   Arnold Kettle: *An Introduction to the English Novel*, vol. I, (Hutchinson: 1951), p. 132.
Chapter Two: Heathcliff (pp. 13–21)
1   Philip Drew: 'Charlotte Brontë as a Critic of *Wuthering Heights*' *Nineteenth Century Fiction*, (1964). Also in Miriam Allott (ed.): *Wuthering Heights: A Selection of Critical Essays*, (Macmillan: 1970) and in Ian Gregor (ed.): *The Brontës: A Collection of Critical Essays* (Prentice-Hall: 1970). Quotations from Gregor, pp. 47 and 50.

2 'The Bridegroom of Barna', in *Blackwood's Edinburgh Magazine*, vol. XLVIII, (November 1840).

Chapter Three: The Lovers (pp. 22–42)

1 Kettle (1951), p. 135.

2 Dorothy van Ghent: *The English Novel; Form and Function*, (Rinehart: 1953, Harper: 1961), p. 157.

3 Terry Eagleton: *Myths of Power: A Marxist Study of the Brontës*, (Macmillan: 1975), p. 108.

4 Derek Traversi: *Wuthering Heights* after a Hundred Years', *Dublin Review*, (1949). Also in Allott (1970), p. 169.

5 Thomas A. Vogler: 'Story and History', in Vogler (1968), p. 10.

6 See *Further Reading* under Heathcliff.

7 The 1939 film version (dir. William Wyler) is probably the fullest articulation of the pure 'romantic' view.

8 Raymond Williams: *The English Novel from Dickens to Lawrence*, (Chatto: 1973), pp. 60–1.

9 Traversi (1949) in Allott (1970), pp. 161, 163.

10 Patricia Meyer Spacks: *The Female Imagination*, (Allen and Unwin: 1976), pp. 138, 150.

11 Eagleton, (1975), p. 101.

12 *Ibid.*, pp. 101–2.

Chapter Four: Language (pp. 42–50)

1 See *Further Reading* under 'Language'.

2 Vogler (1968), p. 15.

3 See *Further Reading* under 'Language'.

4 Arnold Krupat: 'The Strangeness of *Wuthering Heights*', *Nineteenth Century Fiction*, 235 (1970), p. 273.

5 David Musselwhite: '*Wuthering Heights*: The Unacceptable Text', *Red Letters*, 2, (1976), p. 4; reprinted in Francis Barker (et. al., eds.): *Literature, Society and the Sociolgy of Literature*, (University of Essex, (1977).

Chapter Five: Novel or Romance? (pp. 51–62)

1 Northrop Frye: *The Anatomy of Criticism* (Princeton University press: 1957), pp. 304–5.

2 Tom Stoppard: *Rosencrantz and Guildenstern are Dead*(Faber: 1975), pp. 46–7.

3 For 'realism' and 'romance' see *Further reading* under 'Conventions'.

4 See above, Ch. 3, pp. 40–2: and *Further reading* under 'Conventions'.

Chapter Six: Second Generation (pp. 63–70)

1 Q.D.Leavis: 'A Fresh Approach to *Wuthering Heights*', in F.R. and Q.D. Leavis: *Lectures in America* (Chatto: 1969), pp. 128–9.

2 Inga-Stina Ewbank: *Their Proper Sphere: the Brontës as Female Novelists*, (Edward Arnold: 1966), pp. 126–8.

3 Miriam Allott: 'The Rejection of Heathcliff', *Essays in Criticism*, (1959). In allott (1970), p. 205.

4 See *Further reading* under 'Narrative'.

5 See above, Ch. 3, pp. 40–2.

Chapter Seven: Writer and Readers (pp. 71–87)

1 See Winifred Gérin: *Emily Brontë*, (Oxford University Press: 1971), p. 39.

2 See Leavis (1969), p. 127.

3 A.L. Morton: 'Genius on the Border', in *The Matter of Britain: Essays in a Living Culture*, (Lawrence and Wishart: 1966), pp. 124–5.

4 Walter Scott: *Review* of Jane Austen's *Emma* (1815), *Quarterly Review* vol. XIV. Also in Miriam Allott (ed.) *Novelists on the Novel*, (Routledge: 1959), pp. 63–6.

5 Daniel Defoe: 'Preface' to *The History and Remarkable Life of the Truly Honourable Colonel Jacques*(1722).

6 Samuel Richardson: 'Postcript' to *Clarissa, the History of a Young Lady* (1747–8).

7 Henry James (1881) Preface to *The Portrait of a Lady*; first printed in the New York edition of the *Novels and Stories*, (1907–17), vol. IV.

8 See Allott (1970), p. 46, 44, 40, 77, 42.

9 See Penguin *Wuthering Heights*, p. 40.

10 See Ewbank (1966), p. 25.

11 See Allott (1970), p. 48.

12 See above, Ch. 1, p. 1–3.

13 See Ch. 4 above (pp. 49–50). and Ch. 4, note 5

14 Joanna Russ: *How to Suppress Womens' Writing*, (Womens' Press: 1983). See especially pp. 42–3.

15 Elaine Showalter: *A Literature of Their Own*, (Princeton University Press: 1978, Virago: 1978).

16 Sandra Gilbert and Susan Gubar: *The Madwoman in the Attic: the Woman Writer and the Nineteenth-century Literary Imagination*, (Yale University Press: 1979).

Suggestions for further reading

Ideally a 'further reading list' (or, more forbiddingly, a 'select bibliography') should be the beginning of a student's independent work on a text, author or period. This *Guide* has made extensive use of critical writing on *Wuthering Heights*: but as my use of a critic is always specific to a particular point, you won't get from the *Guide* itself much idea of how that critic addresses other questions, or the problems of the novel as a whole. Furthermore, a *Guide* to a specific text can't give the larger general issues it must inevitably raise the attention they require. You will need, in other words, to go yourself directly to books of criticism and theory in order to absorb and evaluate their contributions to our understanding of the text in question and of literature as a whole.

The list that follows is not a comprehensive bibliography of critical works on *Wuthering Heights*; and certainly not an adequate summary of general works available. It is designed rather to guide you into criticism and theory, by presenting a selection of what seem to me the most useful titles, and giving you some idea of their character and value. Only a few titles on larger topics are included: but these works, where indicated, contain their own comprehensive bibliographies on the subjects they address.

The further reading list is sub-divided under headings roughly corresponding to the chapters of the *Guide*.

Texts

I have been referring for convenience throughout this *Guide* to the Penguin English Library edition of *Wuthering Heights*, edited by David Daiches (1965). The standard text is the Oxford University Press Clarendon edition, edited by Ian Jack and Hilda Marsden (OUP, 1976). This text is also available in paperback in the World's Classics series (OUP, 1981). The chief advantage in using a modern edited text such as those of Daiches and Jack, is that they base their editorial readings on the first edition of *Wuthering Heights* (London: Thomas Newby, 1847), the only text to appear in Emily Brontë's lifetime. Many subsequent editions followed Charlotte Brontë's 1850 revision of the text, (London: Smith, Elder, 1850), which succeeded in correcting many printer's errors, but also altered the text in matters of paragraphing and punctuation, and toned down some of the language and dialogue by softening their rough and regional character. Modern editors agree on the importance of establishing a text which reflects as accurately as possible the author's intentions, by basing their editions on the text of 1847.

Narrative

The unusual narrative method of *Wuthering Heights* understandably attracted critical attention, at least from the 1950s. Lockwood's role as narrator was examined in a series of articles in the journal *Nienteenth Century Fiction*: Carl Woodring in 'The Narrators of *Wuthering Heights*' (NCF, 11, 1957) argued that Lockwood should be regarded as a 'sentimentalist'; George J. Worth ('Emily Brontë's Mr Lockwood', NCF, 12, 1958) proposed a more ironical reading of the character. Edgar F. Shannon, Jr, established the importance of Lockwood's nightmares in 'Lockwood's dreams and the exegesis of *Wuthering Heights*', (NCF, 14, 1959); and J.K. Mathison ventured the interesting suggestion that Nelly is an unreliable narrator in 'Nelly Dean and the Power of *Wuthering Heights*', (NCF, 11, 1956).

These articles of the 1950s belong to the school of American 'New Criticism': they are essentially descriptive and formalistic, concerned exclusively with the internal properties of literary works. Our contemporary interest in narrative is sustained rather by those modern developments in both the theory and practice of fiction discussed in Chapters 4 and 6. Many works of 'post-modernist' fiction have broken with the traditions of 'realistic', represent-ational writing; and simultaneously literary criticism has developed a corresponding concern with the theoretical complexities involved in the relations between literature and 'real life'. Some pioneering work along these lines was done in the Soviet Union in the 1930s by a group of theoreticians who came to be known as the 'Russian Formalists'. An introduction to their work, and to much contemporary theorizing about literature, can be found in Tony Bennett's *Formalism and Marxism* (London: Methuen, 1979). You will find a comprehensive account of narrative strategies in Shlomoth Rimmon-Kenan: *Narrative Fiction: Contemporary Poetics* (London: Methuen, 1983). The isues about narrative I raised in Chapter 6 can be followed up in Patricia Waugh: *Metafiction: the Theory and Practice of Self-Conscious Fiction* (London: Methuen, 1984). Both Waugh and Rimmon-Kennan have excellent bibliographies.

Heathcliff

You will find different and illuminating views of Heathcliff in the works already cited by Kettle (1951), Traversi (1949), van Ghent (1953), Leavis (1969) and Eagleton (1975). The problem of 'sympathy' and the use of narrative point-of-view to control the reader's responses, are discussed in John Hagan: 'Control of Sympathy in *Wuthering heights*', (*Nineteenth Century Fiction*, 21, 1967). Heathcliff's relation to Romanticism (see below) and the 'Gothic' conventions are described by Jacques Blondel in 'Literary Influences on *Wuthering heights*', in Allott, (1970). There is a good descriptive study of the 'Byronic hero' figure in Mario Praz: *The Romantic Agony*, (trans. Angus Davidson, 2nd ed., London: Oxford University Press, 1951).

My discussion of Heathcliff also raise questions about 'realism' and the powers of literature to invoke both the 'real' and the 'unreal' within its imagined worlds. You will find a full and fascinating account of the various techniques available to writers for evoking the 'unreal', and employing non-realistic discourses to interrogate convention, orthodox thinking and reductive conceptions of 'reality', in Rosemary Jackson: *Fantasy: the Literature of Subversion*, (London: Methuen, 1981).

The lovers

Most of the criticism which deals usefully with the 'love' theme of *Wuthering Heights* has already been cited in Chapter 3. There is also a very interesting eassy by Mark Kinkead-Weeks: 'The Place of Love in *Jane Eyre* and *Wuthering Heights*', in Ian Gregor (ed.): *The Brontës: a Collection of Critical Essays*, (Prentice-Hall, 1970), which relates the love-theme to aspects of narrative point-of-view, the contrast between the two houses, and other features of the novel's technique.

If you are interested in following up any of the different theoretical views outlined in Chapter 3, the following list should provide a beginning. Keith Odom in 'The Brontës and Romantic Views of Personality', (*Dissertation Abstracts*, 22, 1961), gives a good account of the novel's 'romantic' features. The 'historical' view is best represented by the works already cited: Kettle (1951), Williams (1973) and Eagleton (1975). Some works which set the novel into a historical context are mentioned below, under *Writer and Readers*. A 'religious' approach to Emily Brontë's work is adopted by G.D. Klingopolous in '*Wuthering Heights*: the Novel as Dramatic Poem', (*Scrutiny*, 14, 1947); which deals with Emily's poetry. A considerable amount of psychoanalytic criticism appeared in the 1950s and 60s: commencing perhaps with Richard Chase: 'The Brontës:A Centennial Observance', (*Kenyon Review*, IX, 1947), (also in Gregor, 1970): and following by Eric Solomon: 'The Incest Theme in *Wuthering Heights*', (*Nineteenth Century Fiction*, 14, 1959): Wade Thompson: 'Infanticide and Sadism in *Wuthering Heights*', (*PMLA*, 78, 1963); and Thomas Moser: 'What is the Matter with Emily Jane? Conflicting Impulses in *Wuthering Heights*', (*Nineteenth Century Fiction*, 17, 1962). For feminist criticism, see below under *Contemporary criticism*.

Language

There has been little work on the linguistic aspects of *Wuthering Heights*, except for some specialized articles on the use of Yorkshire dialect. Robert C. McKibben's 'The Image of the Book in *Wuthering Heights*', (*Nineteenth Century Fiction*, 15, 1960), (also in Gregor, 1970), examines the foregrounding of 'language' and 'literature' as concepts in the novel. The best recent general book on the application of linguistic science to novel criticism is Roger

Fowler: *Linguistics and the Novel* (London: Methuen, 1970), which also contains an excellent bibliography of works on linguistics, linguistic criticism, structuralist analysis of narrative, and theory of fiction.

Conventions

'Romanticism' is a very large and complex subject which has occupied many pages of theoretical debate. Early attempts to define Romanticism postulated 'the romantic' as a permanent character-istic of human consciousness (sometimes opposed to the 'classic' temper or form); but Romanticism is best understood in relation to the cultural movements of the late eighteenth and early nineteenth centuries which produced, out of a period of historical revolution, influential new forms of expression. A recent general introduction to the period can be found in Marilyn Butler: *Romantics, Rebels and Reactionaries* (Oxford University Press, 1981). More theoretical definitions are attempted in David Thorburn and Geoffrey Hartman (eds.): *Romanticism* (Cornell University Press, 1973); and in Northrop Frye: *Romanticism Reconsidered*, (Columbia University Press, 1963).

'Realism' is also a term of great theoretical difficulty and the ground of much philosophical argument. The earliest theorists of realism in the novel were its practitioners, the French novelists Balzac and Zola, who developed a theory of fiction as the imitator of living history. This 'mimetic' view of the realist novel as a representational form is discussed with a wealth of illustration in Erich Auerbach: *Mimesis*, (1946; Princeton University Press, 1953; Anchor Books, 1957); and in Georg Lukacs: *Studies in European Realism*, (London: Highway Publishing, 1950). Recent criticism has challenged this mimetic view of realism; you can pursue some of these developments in Catherine Belsey: *Critical Practice* (London: Methuen, 1980). For a different view of 'realism' you might consult Damien Grant: *Realism* (Methuen, 1970).

Biography

As there is no contemporary biography of Emily Brontë, the best first-hand account is Elizabeth Gaskell's *Life of Charlotte Brontë*, (London: Smith, Elder, 1857). Study of the Brontë juvenilia produced interesting biographical interpretations in Fanny Ratchford's *The Brontë's Web of Childhood* (New York:

Columbia University Press, 1941) and *Gondal's Queen* (Austin, Texas: University of Texas Press, 1955), which link the mature writings back to the children's literary apprenticeship. Mary Visick pursued the same line in *The Genesis of Wuthering Heights* (1960; 3rd edition, London: Ian Hodgkins, 1980). John Hewish examines life and works in *Emily Brontë: A Critical and Biographical Study*, (London: MacMillian, 1969); and Lynne Reid Banks has written a readable fictionalization in *Dark Quartet* (London: Weidenfeld and Nicolson, 1976). The standard biography of Emily is Winifred Gérin (Oxford University Press: 1971).

The historical background is explored in the essay cited by A.L. Morton, and in David Wilson: 'Emily Brontë: First of the Moderns', in *Modern Quarterly Literary Miscellany*, (London: Lawrence and Wishart, 1947). Tom Winnifrith's *The Brontës and their Background* (London: MacMillan, 1973) is the best full-length study of the writers in their historical context. The books by Winnifrith and Eagleton (1975) refer to many useful works of a more formally historiographical nature.

Contemporary criticism

A good short introduction to structuralism and its impact on literary criticism and theory is Terry Hawkes: *Structuralism and Semiotics*, (London: Methuen, 1977). You might also consult Ann Jefferson and David Robey: *Modern Literary Theory: A Comparative Introduction*, (London: Batsford, 1982). The bibliographies of Hawkes (1977), Belsey (1980), Waugh (1984) and Bennett (1979) will furnish you with a comprehensive list of works dealing with the complexities of contemporary literary theory and criticism. I have discussed feminist criticism of *Wuthering Heights* in Chapter 7; there are many general works on literature form a feminist perspective, but you might begin with Kate Millett's *Sexual Politics* (London: Hart-Davis, 1971; Virago, 1978); and Germaine Greer's *The Female Eunuch* (St. Alban's: Paladin, 1971). A full-length post-structuralist study, esoteric but impressive, can be found in James H. Kavanagh: *Emily Brontë* (Blackwell, 1985).

Index